Creating Literacy-Based Programs for Children

Creating Literacy-Based Programs for Children

Lesson Plans and
Printable Resources for K–5

R. LYNN BAKER

An imprint of the American Library Association

CHICAGO 2017

R. Lynn Baker is an early childhood educator and certified librarian. A former preschool and kindergarten teacher, she holds a bachelor of science degree in interdisciplinary early childhood education with a minor in special education. Lynn spent eight years as a youth services librarian, developing programs and curricula for children, families, and communities in the public library, and received her MLIS degree from San José State University. Lynn is an early childhood and public library consultant, providing workshops for early care and education organizations and library systems. Lynn currently lives in Frankfort, Kentucky, with her husband, Andrew, and their two sons, Thomas and Tyler.

© 2017 by the American Library Association

Extensive effort has gone into ensuring the reliability of the information in this book; however, the publisher makes no warranty, express or implied, with respect to the material contained herein.

ISBN: 978-0-8389-1500-4 (paper)

Library of Congress Cataloging-in-Publication Data

Names: Baker, R. Lynn, author.
Title: Creating literacy-based programs for children : lesson plans and printable
    resources for K-5 / R. Lynn Baker.
Description: Chicago : ALA Editions, an imprint of the American Library
    Association, 2017.
Identifiers: LCCN 2016047914 | ISBN 9780838915004 (pbk. : alk. paper)
Subjects: LCSH: Children's libraries—Activity programs. | Children's
    libraries—Activity programs—United States. | Literacy—Study and
    teaching (Primary)—Activity programs. | Literacy—Study and teaching
    (Elementary)—Activity programs.
Classification: LCC Z718.3 .B34 2017 | DDC 027.62/5—dc23 LC record available
    at https://lccn.loc.gov/2016047914

Book design by Kim Thornton in the Freight Text Pro, Freight Sans Pro, and Archer typefaces. Cover images © Shutterstock, Inc.

♾ This paper meets the requirements of ANSI/NISO Z39.48–1992 (Permanence of Paper).

Printed in the United States of America
21 20 19 18 17   5 4 3 2 1

For Andrew, Thomas, and Tyler

Contents

Literacy and Reading Skills by Grade and Developmental Stages

THE PUBLIC LIBRARY'S OVERALL GOAL IS TO PROMOTE LITERacy and a love of reading. The goal of programs for children should be no different. In order to plan meaningful programs that foster literacy skills for children, it is important that you understand the foundational skills that are required for a child to become a successful reader. Reading skills begin long before a child begins reading. These early literacy skills set the foundation for a child to build upon when she enters kindergarten. From kindergarten through fifth grade, children continue to grow as readers. From learning how to decode words to reading fluently, it is during this time that children move from learning how to read to reading to learn.

In this chapter, we will take a look at the stages of reading—beginning with early literacy skills and moving through the final stages of comprehension and fluency. We will also take a look at the foundational principles and stages of childhood development that impact growth of reading skills. This foundational understanding of reading is meant to help you build more intentional and impactful programs for children in kindergarten through fifth grade.

Early Literacy Skills

If you provide programs for preschool children at your library, then you are likely familiar with the term *early literacy*. In essence, early literacy skills are those skills that a child must develop before he learns to read on his own. In order to understand how to build literacy-rich programs for children in kindergarten through fifth grade, it is important to understand the principles of early literacy development. Six early literacy skills provide the basis for the Every Child Ready to Read initiative, which was developed by the Public Library Association and the Association for Library Service to Children.[1]

SIX EARLY LITERACY SKILLS

Print awareness is a child's first step toward reading as she recognizes text that is printed on the page and the fact that the text has meaning.

Letter knowledge is a child's understanding that each letter has different physical characteristics, has a unique name, and makes different sounds. A child with letter knowledge also has the ability to recognize and name individual letters.

Phonological awareness is a child's understanding that words are made up of smaller, individual sounds.

Print motivation is a child's interest in and enjoyment of reading.

Narrative skills are exhibited by a child's ability to retell a story in the correct sequence.

Vocabulary skills refer to a child's ability to connect words to objects, people, and places in the world around him.

FIVE BEST PRACTICES OF EVERY CHILD READY TO READ

Effective early childhood programs foster the early literacy skills just described through the use of five best practices that are interwoven throughout the program in order to intentionally support the development of each of the six early literacy skills. These best practices are at the center of the second edition of Every Child Ready to Read, which was released in 2011.[2]

Talking includes expressive and receptive language, which is displayed through verbal and auditory communication. Talking is an important indicator of later success in reading.

Singing slows down the sounds in language and combines with rhythm and rhyme to help prepare children for the sounds and rhythms that are a part of reading.

Reading includes being read to at an early age. This process includes asking the child questions about the story as well. Answering questions about the story helps children prepare for learning how to navigate stories on their own.

Writing skills begin before a child can write one word. A child develops fine muscle control and writing skills through practicing drawing and coloring before learning how to form letters on her own.

Playing is a child's work. Children learn important language skills through social play with adults and peers. Play should also incorporate printed text as much as possible in order to expose children to printed words prior to reading. This practice includes the use of familiar logos and signs, also known as environmental print, which is often a child's first step toward independent reading.

As children move from practicing early literacy skills to reading text on their own, they will build on new skills in order to master more advanced levels of independent reading. These new skills are interrelated and are connected to early literacy skills and practices. Strong early literacy skills, particularly phonological awareness and vocabulary skills, are usually good predictors of strong reading skills. It is important that children continue to expand these skills in order to become strong, independent readers. In particular, phonemic awareness and vocabulary skills provide the building blocks required for developing the comprehension and fluency skills needed to become a successful reader.

Beginning Readers

Most kindergarten through primary grade–level children who attend your programs will be at the beginning of their journey as readers. Children who have been exposed to early literacy practices prior to kindergarten will connect more easily with the skills needed to become strong readers. These skills build on the six early literacy skills we covered earlier in this chapter.

Decoding builds on phonological awareness skills. It is a child's ability to quickly combine individual letter sounds (phonemes) within a word to accurately read and pronounce the entire word.[3] If a child struggles with decoding words, it will be difficult for that child to be successful with the other skills needed for reading. Program activities that foster decoding skills for young readers include phonics-based games, activities that play with letter sounds, rhyming games, group reading activities, and the like. More specific activities can be found in chapter 10, which includes a variety of lesson plans meant to guide your elementary school–age program planning.

Comprehension is a child's ability to read and understand the meaning of text. Comprehension of text is directly impacted by the child's prior knowledge and experiences. A new reader will struggle with understanding text that is not connected to real-life experiences. Children who are exposed to diverse vocabulary in language-rich environments, and those who have a broader range of experiences, will develop stronger comprehension skills because they are able to connect more of what they are reading to the real world. It is important for new readers to be exposed to other cultures and global ideas that may not be a direct part of their own world, so that they are familiar with diverse practices and experiences. This is one reason that it is important to expose children to experiences that are multiculturally diverse during library programs for young readers.

Fluency is a more advanced reading skill and is a child's ability to read text with speed and expression.[4] A child who reads fluently is able to make sense of the text that she reads (comprehension) without making many mistakes. Oral fluency practice (also known as reading aloud) helps the beginning reader with silent reading fluency as well. Research shows a connection between fluency and a child's ability to comprehend what she reads, whether aloud or silently.[5]

These beginning reading skills will continue to grow for most children throughout the primary grades. Writing and spelling skills are also dependent on the foundational literacy skills that were covered earlier in this chapter. As a child advances as a reader during the early primary years, his writing skills also begin to develop. It is important to support beginning readers through activities that offer opportunities to practice these skills. As children become stronger readers, the types of activities that you offer must broaden in order to foster more advanced skills. Children in third through fifth grade (commonly referred to as *tweens*) will typically advance to an intermediate level of reading skills and will be ready for activities that connect with more abstract concepts.

Intermediate Readers

Most children in the third through fifth grades have spent several years learning how to read and are becoming intermediate readers. It is usually at this point that the purpose of literacy development shifts from learning to read toward reading to learn. Reading becomes more purposeful, and children are able to comprehend more abstract concepts and ideas. At this stage of reading, a child is able to navigate through more difficult vocabulary, descriptive devices, and language mechanics. Children begin to develop the ability to decipher the meaning of unfamiliar words from context clues that are provided by other words within the text.[6] All other academic areas become more closely tied to a child's ability to read and make sense of information. Writing and spelling skills continue to mature and are connected to a child's expressive language skills. Written language skills become more advanced as children are able to control more of their own thought processes.

In order to foster a love of reading among intermediate readers, it is important that children have the opportunity to read books for enjoyment. For programming librarians, providing this opportunity means that programs must include enjoyable activities that encourage reading while also connecting to the development of age-appropriate literacy skills. These developing skills work in tandem with a child's interest in reading. The level of success a child experiences with each of these skills impacts the child's motivation and desire to read more on her own. Reading skills during this stage build on the comprehension and fluency skills that were developed earlier. These skills correspond with the following abstract thinking skills that are a part of independent reasoning and problem solving.

Metacognition refers to a child's awareness of his own thoughts as he reads. Metacognition involves self-regulating comprehension strategies such as silent self-questioning, summarizing, and predicting what will happen based on making inferences.[7] The use of these tools helps the child connect to and make sense of what he is reading.

Executive functions allow children to focus attention and act on information. The executive function skills include activation, focus, effort, emotional connection, working memory, and self-monitoring.[8]

During the *activation* stage of reading, children prepare to concentrate on what they will be reading. This level of concentration is needed for comprehension and is often a lengthier process when reading for academic reasons rather than reading for enjoyment based on motivational factors and interest levels. When it is time to read, a child must be able to *focus* in order to comprehend what she is reading. The *effort* that the child puts forth while reading the text is linked to her ability to sustain focus, her level of interest, and her *emotional connection* to the text. All these executive functions impact the child's motivation to continue reading.

Another executive function, *working memory,* is required for retaining information as a child reads. This means that when a child reads, he has to hold on to the information that he has already read and connect it to new information as he continues reading.

As a child matures as an active reader, she develops an awareness of how well she is comprehending and remembering what she is reading. At this stage, the reader is able to self-regulate, or *self-monitor,* by shifting strategies as needed. This self-awareness helps the child engage with, retain, and comprehend what she is reading. A child at this stage of reading is also capable of recognizing when a word in the text is unfamiliar and is usually able to decipher its meaning through context clues provided by familiar words within the same sentence. Mature readers are able to retain the meaning of newly learned words, a skill that is needed for children to build new literacy skills.

Developmental Considerations

In addition to understanding literacy development, it is important to understand the developmental stages that children move through as they work to become independent readers. Many factors related to a child's development impact literacy skills and the development of reading comprehension skills. The foundation should be established prior to a child's entrance into kindergarten because the most crucial period of brain development occurs during the first five years of life.[9] Most states have adopted a definition of kindergarten readiness based on a list of common early childhood characteristics that are needed for success in kindergarten.[10] These indicators of readiness include approaches to learning, cognition and general knowledge, physical well-being and motor development, social and emotional development, and language development.[11]

> *Approaches to learning*: A child's interest in and enthusiasm for learning
>
> *Cognition and general knowledge*: Mathematical reasoning and imaginative thinking
>
> *Physical well-being and motor development*: A child's level of health, including muscle movement and development
>
> *Social and emotional development*: The ability to interact appropriately with others and the ability to regulate one's own emotions
>
> *Language development*: The ability to communicate through verbal, written, or physical means. Language development is connected to literacy development and includes vocabulary and communication skills

Children who have developed these skills feel more confident and become more successful learners and readers in kindergarten. As a child enters school, several internal factors impact the way the child learns, including social and emotional skills, cognitive reasoning skills, personality traits, and individual learning styles.

SOCIAL AND EMOTIONAL SKILLS

The social and emotional skills of children in kindergarten through second grade play a significant role in the development of literacy and other academic skills. A child who feels confident and secure struggles less.[12] Self-regulation, or a child's ability to understand and control his own emotions and impulses, allows him to focus on learning. This skill is exhibited through a child's ability to wait her turn, share with others, and give and take when working with peers. Children who have developmentally appropriate social and emotional skills in early elementary school are able to build and sustain friendships and are able to work independently when needed.[13] The ability (or inability) to work independently and follow directions has a meaningful effect on reading. If a child struggles with working independently, he will struggle with silent reading and comprehension as well. Conversely, if a child does not feel like she belongs socially within her group of peers, she will most likely struggle with learning as well.

During the period between third and fifth grade, children become more concerned with belonging socially.[14] Children at this age are able to understand and create social rules. Self-awareness skills also begin to develop at this stage, and children are capable of understanding that their choices have consequences. Decision making begins to mature, and children begin making decisions with personal responsibility and consequences in mind. In addition, children during their tween years begin to seek out information and opportunities for learning. This process is known as *mastery orientation,* a skill that is tied to growth in reliance on personal responsibility rather than dependence on receiving accolades from others.[15] This intrinsic motivation to learn is best fostered by opportunities in which children are challenged yet also have the ability to succeed. It is important that library programs support this stage through developmentally appropriate, literacy-based activities that are enjoyable but also challenging.

Although library programs usually incorporate whole-group activities, independent activities should also be included whenever possible. Examples of independent activities in library programs may include independent reading at home in preparation for book discussion groups, individual completion of a part of a group project, or even computer gaming as children work independently on individual computers. More specific activities to help foster self-regulation skills can be found in the lesson plan chapter of this book.

COGNITIVE REASONING SKILLS

As children enter kindergarten, they begin to notice more of the world around them. Prior to age six, children's thoughts are more egocentric, focusing on their own needs and wants. During this new stage, cognitive skills expand, and children are able to think about other people and how the world works. Children in early elementary school begin to reason and think logically based on new knowledge and experiences.[16] Problem-solving skills become more advanced, and children are able to apply abstract thinking to create alternative solutions.

At this point in their development, children are also able to express their cognitive thoughts through more advanced language and other modes of communication, including speaking, writing, and creating through digital means. It is important to provide opportunities for children to express themselves in order to support language and cognitive skills through a variety of media (which we will cover in more depth in the following chapter on multiliteracies). Meaningful library programs offer activities that allow tweens to express their thoughts through talking, writing, and digital creations, as well as through social experiences with peers.

PERSONALITY TRAITS

As a child matures, his personality continues to develop. The type of learner he becomes is heavily dependent on the characteristics of his temperament.[17] A child may do well with transitions and take to new situations easily, or he may be slow to warm up to new people, places, or ideas. Strong-willed children may be more assertive during social learning activities, while a child who is more introverted may need time for quiet reflection. It is important to remember that not all children learn, think, or interact in the same way, and program activities should be planned with different personality needs in mind.

> *Easygoing* children are generally flexible and deal with transitions and new experiences without much trouble. However, it is also important to remember that just because a child's demeanor appears easygoing on the surface does not mean that she is also outgoing or that any and all types of programs will work for her. It is very possible that an easygoing child may also have a more introverted personality which requires that the child have time to warm up to new people. No one personality trait makes up the whole of a child's temperament.
>
> *Slow-to-warm-up* children need time to acclimate to new surroundings, people, and experiences. They may position themselves just outside the group, observing without actively participating.[18] It is important to remember that just because a child may not look actively engaged doesn't mean that he isn't participating. Some children simply need to be active listeners for a while before becoming active participants.
>
> *Strong-willed* children are usually more intense in nature. They often dive right in to new experiences without much need for transition time; however, they also tend to be more sensitive when faced with social conflicts.[19] Strong-willed children are usually quite intelligent and do well in leadership roles that keep them actively engaged. This trait also usually means that the strong-willed child is outgoing, but a strong-willed child may also need time to herself for independent thinking because strong-willed children may be easily distracted.

This short list of learning styles is by no means exhaustive. A child's temperament may be more in line with one of these personality types or may be a combination of them. It is important to get to know children who regularly attend your programs. This awareness can help you plan the best experiences possible for a variety of learning styles and personalities. Although you may not be able to perfectly align every part of your program with every type of personality that might attend, when you make an effort to get to know the children who regularly attend your programs, you are able to make adjustments as needed. This ability to adjust increases the likelihood that your program will make a positive impact on the children who attend.

INDIVIDUAL LEARNING STYLES

In addition to personality traits, children exhibit different types of learning styles that impact the way they take in information. These same learning styles are common in adults as well. As libraries plan programs for children—and for adults who may attend programs with their children—including activities that appeal to each type of learner helps produce success.

Most group learning is designed for the *visual learner*. True visual learners need to be able to see something to understand it.[20] For programming, accommodating this trait means using visual representations to relay information. Such representations might include pictures, videos, slide presentations, or props. In programs that involve more discussion, visual learners often like to look at something to help them concentrate. For some children, this predilection might mean drawing doodles on scrap paper or making a craft while they listen. If a program will include a hands-on project, the visual learner will benefit from seeing a physical representation of the process beforehand. Programmers might choose to walk through an example for children or show a video of the process to help visual learners.

An *auditory learner* learns best through listening and discussing what he is learning. The auditory learner does best when activity instructions are given verbally. Visual or written explanations do not offer much help to a child who is an auditory learner; he needs to hear explanations in order to retain them. Information that is spoken makes the most sense to the auditory learner, and reading aloud and discussing text help the auditory learner retain what he reads. He may need to talk aloud to himself or others in order to work through the steps of an activity.

The *kinesthetic learner* learns best through movement and tactile activities. She solves problems through physical manipulation and often expresses her thoughts through physical movements and gestures. Hands-on activities provide opportunities for the kinesthetic learner to interact with materials, which help her learn from her own actions. For children who learn best by doing, it is not enough to simply provide written or spoken instructions. Public library programs help children who are kinesthetic learners connect to the world around them by allowing them to practice doing what they are reading and learning about. Programs that incorporate hands-on activities—such as arts and crafts, scientific experiments, technology-based learning, or real-world building and engineering practices—best support the needs of the kinesthetic learner. For more programming ideas that are linked to the various learning styles, be sure to read the lesson plan chapter of this book.

As we have covered in this chapter, a variety of developmental and individual considerations should be taken into account when creating programs for children in kindergarten through fifth grade. From reading skill development to social and emotional development, cognitive abilities, and learning styles, the public library's overall goal is to promote literacy and a love of reading through programs that challenge children to learn more. In addition to promoting developmental growth, the twenty-first-century library connects programs to multiple types of literacies, including social, language and communication, technology and media, and information literacies. Also known as *multiliteracies,* these areas of modern information communication involve more than simply reading text. The next chapter defines each area of multiliteracy and its importance to the twenty-first-century learner.

NOTES

1. Elaine Meyers and Harriet Henderson, "Overview of Every Child Ready to Read @ your library, 1st Edition," Every Child Ready to Read @ your library, www.everychild readytoread.org/project-history%09/overview-every-child-ready-read-your-library %C2%AE-1st-edition.

2. Saroj Ghoting, "The Five Practices and the Early Literacy Components Support Each Other," www.earlylit.net/ecrtr/.

3. National Institute for Literacy, "Key Literacy Component: Decoding," AdLit.org, www.adlit.org/article/27875/.

4. "Fluency," Reading Rockets, www.readingrockets.org/teaching/reading101/fluency.

5. Peter Fisher, "Learning about Literacy: From Theories to Trends," *Teacher Librarian,* 35, no. 3 (2008): 8–12.

6. Common Core State Standards Initiative, "English Language Arts Standards—Reading: Foundational Skills," www.corestandards.org/ELA-Literacy/RF/.

7. Regina Boulware-Gooden, Suzanne Carreker, Ann Thornhill, and R. Malatesha Joshi, "Instruction of Metacognitive Strategies Enhances Reading Comprehension and Vocabulary Achievement of Third-Grade Students," Reading Rockets, www.reading rockets.org/article/instruction-metacognitive-strategies-enhances-reading -comprehension-and-vocabulary.

8. Linda R. Hecker, "The Reading Brain: Executive Function Hard at Work," Learning Disabilities Association of America, http://ldaamerica.org/the-reading-brain -executive-function-hard-at-work/.

9. Center on the Developing Child, Harvard University, "In Brief: The Science of Early Childhood Development," http://developingchild.harvard.edu/resources/inbrief-science-of-ecd/.

10. U.S. Department of Education, "Definitions," www.ed.gov/early-learning/elc-draft-summary/definitions.

11. R. Lynn Baker, *Counting Down to Kindergarten: A Complete Guide to Creating a School Readiness Program for Your Community* (Chicago, IL: ALA Editions, 2015).

12. Robert Brooks and Sam Goldstein, *Raising Resilient Children: Fostering Strength, Hope, and Optimism in Your Child* (Baltimore, MD: Paul H. Brooks, 2002).

13. M. L. Nichols, *The Parent Backpack for Kindergarten through Grade 5: How to Support Your Child's Education, End Homework Meltdowns, and Build Parent-Teacher Connections* (New York: Ten Speed Press, 2013).

14. Ibid.

15. "Measuring Elementary School Students' Social and Emotional Skills: Providing Educators with Tools to Measure and Monitor Social and Emotional Skills That Lead to Academic Success," Child Trends, www.childtrends.org/wp-content/uploads/2014/08/2014-37CombinedMeasuresApproachandTablepdf1.pdf.

16. Child Development Institute, "Stages of Intellectual Development in Children and Teenagers," http://childdevelopmentinfo.com/child-development/piaget/.

17. Nichols, *The Parent Backpack for Kindergarten through Grade 5.*

18. Barbara F. Meltz, "A Slow-to-Warm-Up Child Needs Time to Gain Confidence," *Boston Globe,* April 21, 2005, www.boston.com/yourlife/home/articles/2005/04/21/a_slow_to_warm_up_child_needs_time_to_gain_confidence/?page=full.

19. Maureen D. Healy, "The Highly Sensitive (and Stubborn) Child," *Creative Development* (blog), *Psychology Today,* January 7, 2013, https://www.psychologytoday.com/blog/creative-development/201301/the-highly-sensitive-and-stubborn-child.

20. Fiona Baker, "Learning Styles in Children," Kidspot, www.kidspot.com.au/school/primary/learning-and-behaviour/learning-styles-in-children.

2

Multiliteracies Defined

MULTILITERACY IS A NEWER TERM THAT HAS COME ABOUT in response to the diverse ways we communicate with one another in the twenty-first century. Born into the world as digital natives, children need to be able to navigate through many different modes of information retrieval and delivery. In this chapter, we will take a look at five different modes of literacy defined as *multiliteracies*. We will consider ways in which multiliteracies should be addressed within library programs for children in kindergarten through fifth grade in order to best meet the literacy development needs of the whole child.

Five Modes of Multiliteracy

Most information is communicated visually for the typically developing child. This communication mode involves deciphering meaning not only from pictures and graphics but also from text, digital media, social cues, and informational systems. This fundamental skill places visual literacy at the center of all other literacy development. Notice in figure 2.1 (page 14) that each of the four other literacies overlaps with visual literacy. Let's take a look at each type of literacy and examine how children learn to read through mastery of each area.

VISUAL LITERACY

Visual literacy is essential to the typical child's ability to evaluate and make sense of information. Visual elements are part of the modern fabric of human communication across most societies and cultures throughout the world. Textual, digital and media, and information literacy are all connected to a child's

FIGURE 2.1
The Five Modes of Multiliteracy

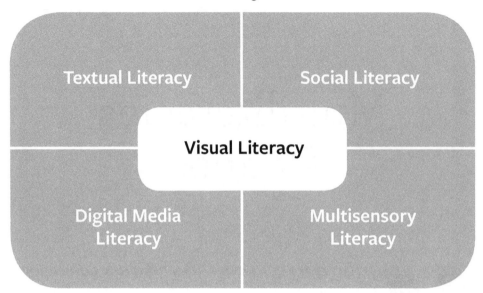

ability to visually find, interpret, and use information that is being communicated, whether it be through text, pictures, or symbols. Social literacy is also tied to a child's ability to interpret visual information. This form of literacy includes a child's understanding of social rules and cues that may be unspoken or conveyed primarily through body language and facial expressions. If a child is unable to comprehend what is being communicated socially through visual means, his social literacy development is likely to be delayed.

A child's ability to interpret visual information is also dependent on real-life experiences and her cultural environment.[1] In order for a child to comprehend the meaning of abstract visual symbols, she must be exposed to the symbols or have experiences that are associated with those symbols. If a symbol is not associated with any previous knowledge, a child will need support in order to comprehend its meaning.[2] Such support translates into providing experiences through programming that expose children to environmental print, such as signs, labels, and logos for beginning readers, and that reinforce previous exposure. This support also relates to a child's ability to translate information from illustrations in order to tell what is happening in the text of a story. Although this ability should begin as a foundational early literacy skill, it is a skill that continues to develop as children work on building inference skills needed for reading comprehension. It is important that programs continue to provide activities that support visual literacy skill development for beginning readers, including the use of picture books, photos, videos, and other visual representations of information. Such activities provide the foundational understanding needed for children to develop a more advanced level of visual comprehension that supports other areas of literacy development, including textual literacy.

TEXTUAL LITERACY

Textual literacy, or reading and synthesizing the printed word, is what most people think of when they think about literacy. Textual literacy pertains to reading and comprehending any form of text, whether it be words in a book, information on a computer screen, or the words and logo on a sign (all visual in nature). In order to foster textual literacy skills in programs for young children, librarians often point out text and illustrations as they read and encourage children to participate by reading familiar text as a group. Library program activities also connect text to building vocabulary skills through conversation and reading. These connections tie textual literacy to social literacy, another mode of multiliteracy that we will discuss later in this chapter. Library programs that incorporate questions related to the text help children build comprehension and fluency skills—the skills needed for a child to master reading.

In addition to supporting the development of reading skills, textual literacy helps develop the skills needed for spelling and writing. In the first chapter we looked at decoding (a child's ability to combine individual letter sounds to accurately read words) as one part of the reading process. The ability to spell involves the reciprocal. *Encoding,* or identifying the individual letter sounds in a spoken word in order to spell the word, represents the expressive form of textual literacy.[3] The ability to put letters together to spell individual words leads to a child's ability to write sentences and, later, paragraphs—important milestones in a child's growth toward writing.

Textual literacy–based programs also connect children to different types of texts. As older children begin reading more advanced texts and accessing information on their own, they become able to discern the purpose of the text, which helps develop more advanced comprehension and information retention skills.[4] For children to become successful readers, they need to be exposed to material that is developmentally appropriate yet also challenging and engaging. This is especially true for reluctant readers, who are not motivated to read unless they enjoy what they are reading. The more a child is interested in what he is reading and the more successful he feels about his own abilities as a reader, the greater the motivation to read more.[5] It is important to cultivate textual literacy and inspire a love of reading through your programs. One way to do both is to create programs that are rich in opportunities for social interaction and discussion.

SOCIAL LITERACY

Social literacy activities can be connected to textual literacy through interactive experiences that are tied to reading, such as dialogic social reading. Conversation and language-building activities are a part of reinforcing reading comprehension and textual literacy. In programs for younger children who have not yet started reading, or for those who are just beginning to read, it is important that conversation be a significant part of the group reading experience. *Dialogic reading,* or interactive reading during which children are asked to answer open-ended questions about text as it is read aloud, promotes print motivation and interest as well as the development of vocabulary and narrative skills.[6] This technique enables young readers to draw on previous knowledge to make predictions about what might happen next in the story. For children who are in the third through fifth grades, dialogic reading can also be incorporated into social activities.[7]

Library programs such as book discussion groups offer a form of dialogic social reading for intermediate readers. Through social interaction with peers and library programming staff, children are able to share their own perspectives and pool their experiences to arrive at conclusions about text. This method supports reading comprehension by allowing children to exchange ideas about what they have read and to share information about their own previous knowledge and experiences.

Social literacy also includes the ability to read cues and understand unspoken social rules and is dependent on what society as a whole defines as *literacy,* based on current social values.[8] The social values of the twenty-first century continue to refine the list of new literacies that are important to cultivate in young readers. Advances in technology and the ways in which we communicate have made the biggest impact on the competencies that young children need to master in order to become literate members of society. Children need to know how to seek, retrieve, and create information through digital means in order to interact with their peers and information. It is important to emphasize online social etiquette as well as Internet safety in library programs that engage children in digital and social media activities.

It is also important that children know how to communicate appropriately in person. Because of the increase in online social interaction, it is important that children understand the differences between in-person and electronic interaction. Program experiences that allow children to engage in social interaction help them develop in-person social skills, such as being respectful, waiting their turn to speak, making eye contact with others when speaking, taking personal responsibility, and reading facial expressions and body language.[9] These skills are important for children to develop in order to communicate effectively and to be able to read social cues from others correctly. Children also need to recognize that specific tones and inflections of spoken language convey meaning. Each of these social literacies can be addressed through social activities in programs. The lesson plans later in this book offer some suggestions for connecting to social literacy development.

DIGITAL MEDIA LITERACY

Digital media literacy encompasses a variety of communication methods that are associated with technology use. This literacy mode includes accessing and creating information that is delivered through electronic means, as well as the ability to communicate effectively through e-mail, social media, and other technology-based platforms. Not all children have access at home to the various digital media systems that exist for their use, so it is especially important that the public library offers resources, access to those resources, and instruction in the appropriate uses of digital media.[10] For children who live in homes without a smartphone, a computer, a tablet, or an Internet connection that allows them access to digital media resources, the public library may be the only place where they can access these resources outside school. Library programs that provide instruction and ample time to experiment with digital media are particularly helpful to children who do not have other opportunities for accessing the technology.

In addition to computer-based media programs, other developmentally appropriate media content—such as Internet-based games, smartphone or tablet applications, video- and music-creating programs, and hands-on "maker" technologies associated with digital resources—offers important tools for elementary school–age children as they begin to develop digital media literacy. It is important that digital media library programs allow children to have hands-on interaction with various types of digital media while also providing person-to-person social interaction. It is also important to remember that, as with all programs, digital media programs should appeal to a variety of learning styles and abilities, attending to the individual learning needs of all participants.

MULTISENSORY LITERACY

Multisensory literacy refers to all the ways in which a child interacts with information and communication through hands-on, active manipulation. This literacy mode connects heavily with a child's individual learning style. Multisensory literacy involves all the child's senses that are appropriate to a given activity (seeing, hearing, touching, smelling, and moving) and helps the child's brain develop tactile, auditory, and visual memories, which, in turn, helps the child retain learned information.[11] In particular, activities that connect to multisensory experiences not only support the learning needs of the kinesthetic learner but also benefit other learning styles, including those of children with special needs. Multisensory literacy–based programs engage children in activities that connect language and reading to various sensorial experiences. Connecting a child's reading comprehension to a sensory-based activity allows the child to experience the text rather than simply read it. This direct participation helps the child commit the information to memory through the sensations experienced while learning the information.

A multisensory experience often used to help children memorize information is the practice of setting words to music. This process can be as simple as singing the alphabet or as complex as making up a simple song to help children remember all fifty states. Music appeals to a child's auditory senses and can be combined with movements or visual cues, or both, in order to enhance the child's ability to retain information. In the same way, other senses might be engaged to help children retain information through hands-on participation.

Although the term *multisensory literacy* may be new to many, the practices behind the terminology have been used in library programs for some time. From art activities that are connected to stories read in programs to the use of music to guide different parts of the program, multisensory experiences have played an important role in library programming. When hands-on activities are intentionally aligned with literacy components, they help make the content of the text real for program participants. Program activities that are purposeful are more likely to have a bigger impact on participants. In the next chapter we will take a look at the purposes behind public library programming for children in kindergarten through fifth grade and how those purposes align with practices that best meet the literacy needs of participants.

NOTES

1. Linda Z. Cooper, "Supporting Visual Literacy in the School Library Media Center: Developmental, Socio-Cultural, and Experiential Considerations and Scenarios," *Knowledge Quest* 36, no. 3 (January/February 2008): 14–19, EBSCOhost Connection.

2. Rebecca McMahon Giles and Karyn Wellhousen Tunks, "Children Write Their World: Environmental Print as a Teaching Tool," *Dimensions of Early Childhood* 38, no. 3 (2010), http://southernearlychildhood.org/upload/pdf/Children_Write _Their_World.pdf.

3. Deborah K. Reed, "Why Teach Spelling?" Reading Rockets, www.reading rockets.org/sites/default/files/Why%20Teach%20Spelling.pdf.

4. National Institute for Literacy, "Key Literacy Component: Text Comprehension," AdLit.org, www.adlit.org/article/27882/.

5. Richard Allington, "The Six Ts of Effective Elementary Literacy Instruction," Reading Rockets, www.readingrockets.org/article/six-ts-effective-elementary-literacy -instruction.

6. Grover J. Whitehurst, "Dialogic Reading: An Effective Way to Read to Preschoolers," Reading Rockets, www.readingrockets.org/article/dialogic-reading-effective-way -read-preschoolers.

7. Fiona Maine, "How Children Talk Together to Make Meaning from Texts: A Dialogical Perspective on Reading Comprehension Strategies," *Literacy* 47, no. 3 (2013): 150–156.

8. Jerome C. Harste, "What Do We Mean by Literacy Now?" *Voices from the Middle* 10, no. 3 (2003), www.readwritethink.org/files/resources/lesson_images/lesson1140/ VM0103What.pdf.

9. Julie Christensen, "Manners Matter! 5 Expert Tips for Teaching Social Skills," Education.com, www.education.com/magazine/article/teaching-social-skills/.

10. Lisa Tripp, "Digital Youth, Libraries, and New Media Literacy," *Reference Librarian* 52, no. 4 (2011): 329–341.

11. Amanda Morin, "Multisensory Instruction: What You Need to Know," Understood, www.understood.org/en/school-learning/partnering-with-childs-school/instructional -strategies/multisensory-instruction-what-you-need-to-know.

What Is
Programming?

WHEN MOST PEOPLE THINK OF PROGRAMS PROVIDED BY public libraries, they often think of baby lapsit programs or storytime programs for toddlers and preschool children and their parents. Unless public libraries adequately advocate for and promote their own programs, the average citizen may not even realize that public libraries also provide programs for entire families, elementary-grade children, tweens, teens, and adults. Although there are many different purposes behind public library programs and services, the underlying goal of all library programming is to connect people with literacy and reading.

Why Do Libraries Provide Programs for Children?

Public libraries have changed over the years, and as they continue to evolve to meet the changing needs of individual communities, programming is becoming a much larger part of their services—children's programming, in particular, has become the cornerstone of growing today's library. When the library connects with young children and maintains a relationship with children and families over time, it is much more likely to cultivate lifelong readers and maintain them as library users. Effective programs bring children into the library and connect them to information, materials, and other library services. Programs for children also cultivate other developmental skills, while providing an opportunity to expand social literacy alongside their peers.

How Do Libraries Create Programs?

Most libraries provide programs for patrons of all ages. There is no standard curriculum for most programs, but libraries that provide programs for children employ programming staff to plan and implement programs. The children's programmer develops, creates, and leads activities and literacy-based programs in the library and out in the community. The children's programmer also works with external presenters to develop special programs for larger events, overseeing and collaborating with presenters to connect events to library materials and services. It is important for the children's programmer to be knowledgeable about child development, literacy skill development, advances in technology, and the current interests of the children being served. It is also important for the children's programmer to be knowledgeable about building community partnerships, event planning, and program marketing techniques.

Meeting the educational and recreational needs and interests of the community is one of the most important ways that the public library remains relevant, and the children's programmer plays a big role in promoting the library and advocating for its place within the community. In addition to developing and presenting programs, it is crucial that the children's programmer be familiar with the children's collection. The programmer promotes books and materials through literacy-rich programming experiences for children. In order to reach the most children, programmers also need to be familiar with other activities within the community and how library programs fit into the overall needs and schedule of the community.

Scheduling Programs

Because most children are in school during the day, and many are involved in multiple after-school activities, planning programs for children during the elementary school years may prove to be a challenge for some libraries. Several strategies can help libraries create programs with content that is of interest, during times that best fit the busy schedules of students and their families. In order to increase the likelihood of program attendance for children in kindergarten through fifth grade, it is important that libraries offer programs during times that not only fit within the programming schedule at the library but also fit the scheduling needs of the potential participants. This coordination means staying up-to-date with school calendars and youth sporting events during each part of the year. One way to keep up is to follow the social media and website pages of schools, parent-teacher organizations, and youth athletic leagues from across the community. If the library gathers as much information as possible from these different areas of the community, the library's program schedule is more likely to work for a larger number of children and families. In addition to following school and sports calendars, it is important for the library to be aware of community homeschool group schedules and any other community-wide activities for families and children. Your library may want to consider developing or joining a community youth council in order to build communication across organizations. Such collaborative committees help build more aligned activities for children and foster collaborative partnerships across the community. Subscribing to community newsletters and the county's newspapers and following the local chamber of commerce can also help ensure that your library has the most accurate information possible. There is a plethora of information to consider, and there is no way to avoid every single overlap with other community programs, but having the best information possible will help your library increase attendance and reach more families.

AFTER-SCHOOL PROGRAMS

Depending on the other events taking place within your community, afternoon or evening is likely to be your library's best option for elementary schoolchildren's programming, especially during the school year. Many types of programs can work during this time of day, and we will take a more specific look at such programs in chapter 5, but it is worth mentioning here that the most successful types of after-school programs at the library are often more recreational in nature. These types of programs may include popular computer or console gaming, card games, or various types of clubs. Other types of programs that work well after school include homework help and tutoring, book discussion groups, readers' theater, and arts and crafts programs.

SATURDAY PROGRAMS

Another scheduling option your library might want to consider is to offer Saturday morning or Saturday afternoon programs. By providing this option, your library is more likely to meet the needs of families who are unable to bring their children to weekday programs at the library. When you plan Saturday programs, you may consider repeating a program that you also offer during the week, allowing patrons to choose between the two. When you plan Saturday programs, keep in mind the same considerations that you use for after-school programs. Ask these questions: What other community events might be happening at the same time? What school-related sporting events are scheduled? Are there other organizations in your community that offer similar programs at this time of day? It is just as important to be aware of other community events when planning Saturday programs as when planning weekday programs.

SCHOOL-BREAK PROGRAMS

School breaks offer another unique opportunity for library programming options. Spring, fall, and holiday breaks make it possible to offer daytime programs for children who are home from school. Long breaks allow you to schedule programs that could meet at the same time each day for a week, such as book clubs or project-based programs that will require more than one day to complete. There is less likelihood of conflicting with school-based activities during breaks, and these times may prove to be perfect for your library to offer continuing daily programs.

Although your program might not have to compete with extracurricular school activities during school breaks, it is important to know what works for your patrons before planning your programs. As with most first attempts at new programming, scheduling may take some trial and error and flexibility on your part. Once you are able to identify what works for your community, your program plans are more likely to prove successful. Your library can directly connect to the scheduling needs of your community before school breaks in several ways, including through surveys.

Surveying the Community

Surveying the community to determine your program schedule is a good first step for planning any program, but it is particularly helpful in planning daily programs, such as those your library might choose to do during school breaks. A variety of methods can be used for surveying the scheduling needs of your community. Depending on feasibility and the connectedness of your library to potential participants, you may choose to develop a paper survey to hand out at the library, at schools, or during outreach programs. There are also a multitude of free online survey and questionnaire builders that enable you to develop your own specific questions, send out e-mail invitations, and post survey links to your library's website or social media page.[1]

As your library develops survey questions related to program scheduling, keep in mind who you would like to target and who will be answering the questions. For gathering information about optimum programming times for children in kindergarten through fifth grade, you will want your survey to target parents and caregivers. The mode of survey delivery will depend on understanding the best system for your community's group of parents. You may find that more parents have the time to complete surveys online, or, depending on the availability of technology access in your community, parents and caregivers may be more likely to complete paper surveys at the library. You will also want to consider making your survey responses anonymous. You can do this with online surveys as well as printed paper surveys. You may find that respondents are more willing to participate and answer accurately without revealing their identity; however, if you will be contacting participants about programs of interest, you may want to consider asking for names and contact information.

The survey questions that you choose to include, no matter which delivery system you select, need to be short and to the point. Conciseness will ensure that more surveys are completed because more parents are likely to complete surveys that are not time consuming. You may choose to use multiple-choice questions if your library has specific program times from which you would like parents to choose. If your program schedule is more flexible, you may want to ask parents open-ended questions or ask them to fill in the times that would work best for their family. While you are gathering information on program times, you may want to include questions about the types of programs that children might be interested in attending. (See the Program Scheduling Survey template in the appendix.)

Passive Programs

Passive programs provide a way to reach more participants on their own times and terms and can be used to collect information about the interests of your library's patrons for future program planning.[2] Passive programs are simple activities that are set up in the children's section of your library. Participants can stop at the area where the activity is set up and participate at any time while they are visiting the library. You may incorporate an activity into your passive program that would collect participant votes for a type or time of an upcoming program. There are many possibilities for collecting informal information through the use of passive programming. We will cover more specific ideas for passive programs in chapter 5. No matter how you collect programming information from patrons, it is important that you connect gathered responses to plans for future programs.

Intentionality

As you gather information about community interests and best timing for programs, remember to tie these factors to the intention behind each program—connecting children to literacy and a love of reading. In chapter 2, we looked at five modes of literacy. It is important to intentionally connect programs to each of these types of literacy development, whether you are planning a book discussion group, a gaming program, or anything in between. It is also critical that you connect your activities to developmental considerations and diverse learning styles in order to connect your programs to the needs and abilities of your participants. It is in making these connections that the effort you make toward building relationships with repeat patrons is invaluable. The more you connect with the needs of your patrons—whether through surveys or informal conversations—the more you are able to build programs that are meaningful to your potential participants. In addition to connecting with potential participants and their parents and caregivers, it is important to support the goals of schools and other child and family services organizations in the community.

Planning Programs That Support Schools and Other Organizations

In addition to being informed about when school and other events are scheduled within the community, the library can support the goals of these events by creating collaborative programs with the sponsoring organizations. One example of a collaborative program that could benefit both a school and the public library is an author visit that is connected to classroom content. The library can contribute financially if feasible and can host author events for area schools. Numerous programs surrounding the author's visit may be planned at the library and other community locations.

Many communities host a collaborative project known as Battle of the Books (http://battleofthebooks.com/). This competition provides reading lists for elementary school students by grade level. Schools come together in a quick-recall match to answer questions on each of the books on their grade-level book lists. Public libraries can support the Battle of the Books competition, or similar book-based competitions, by providing space, books, and organizational leadership.

Public library programs can also support schools that do not have on-campus libraries. These schools may include private schools or alternative schools that do not have funding or space to build a collection or a library media center. Outreach programs can be developed through a collaborative effort between the school and the public library. Cooperative grants for new books can be sought, donations of withdrawn books can be given directly to the school by the library, or, if space is the issue, the library can deliver specific books to support the curriculum at assigned times.

In addition to schools that do not have libraries, many other community organizations provide after-school programs that incorporate literacy and learning. These organizations are often nonprofit and may provide services specifically for children who are at risk. Your library may want to consider developing outreach programs and services for these organizations as well. The children who attend programs such as these are often the children that you will not see in the library because they lack transportation, finances, or parental involvement. Providing outreach programs for at-risk children through collaborative partnerships with after-school programs enables your library to connect with a group of children who may never have visited the library.

When you consider working with underserved populations at schools, after-school programs, or other youth services organizations, it is important to get a feel for what these organizations do and what they really need. Although programmers often have many ideas that are born from library program and event planning experience, there may be new ways that library programming can meet needs that are endemic to the specific organization. Meeting with teachers and leaders from the organization and asking about their vision for a programming partnership may open up brand new programming service opportunities that the library might not have otherwise discovered.

In this chapter we have covered the various purposes of children's library programming, depending on the needs of the participants and collaborative partners. In the next chapter, we will take a closer look at specific types of programs that work well with children in kindergarten through fifth grade.

NOTES

1. Celia Emmelhainz, "Tools for Running Online Surveys in Libraries," *Databrarians* (blog), http://databrarians.org/2015/07/tools-for-running-online-surveys-in-libraries/.

2. Kelly Ireland Rembert, "Reach Your Patrons through Passive Programming," Evanced, http://evancedsolutions.com/passive-programs/.

4

Types of Programs

MANY DIFFERENT TYPES OF PROGRAMS CAN WORK WITH children in kindergarten through fifth grade. Some types of programs can work for all ages within this range with just a simple tweak of the content and activities, while other types work best for specific ages or grades. In this chapter we will take a look at the different types of programs that you may choose to incorporate into your children's programming schedule. It is important to remember that these programs are simply suggestions and should be changed to suit the needs of your library. Many of the programs that are explained in this chapter are also included with specific activity examples in chapter 10.

As you begin the planning process, it is important to remember that your programs need to be developmentally appropriate for the ages and abilities of the children who attend. As you choose the types of programs that you will offer at your library, think about the developmental considerations that we covered in the first chapter. Remember that the core intention of your programs is always to connect children to literacy and learning. It is more important that you make this connection in a way that children enjoy than that you cram in every single activity that you have planned for a program. Following the lead and interests of the children attending your programs will help you meet your overall goal of instilling a love of and interest in reading. If a planned activity or book does not seem to be working, be flexible and willing to change it. When you plan programs, it is a good rule of thumb to have more planned than you can actually do in a program. Extra activities provide backup for those things that you may decide to pull based on the interests of your participants.

As we discussed in chapter 1, children in kindergarten through second grade are just beginning their journey as new readers. Library programs can support this period of growth and learning and need to be sensitive to the varying levels of reading skills of those who attend. Programs that are social in nature and incorporate teamwork help cultivate social and emotional development and can provide opportunities for peer-to-peer modeling of reading skills. When possible, some connection to the written word should be incorporated. Children in third through fifth grade are continuing to develop the ability to comprehend and analyze what they read. The tween years are an important time to offer programs that connect directly to the interests of the children that your library serves. Tweens are beginning to grow socially and have many more activities that compete for their time. It is crucial that your library programs connect to continued literacy skill growth through methods that are viewed as fun and interesting by the tweens that you serve.

Many types of programs can work for both groups of children in elementary school. Some programs may be more suited for children who are attending on their own, while others may be well suited for families that are attending together, but many can work well for either age group.

Club Programs

Several types of programs can work well in the form of ongoing clubs for children in kindergarten through second grade or tweens in third through fifth grade. Crafting clubs can be scheduled once a week with rotating themes or once a month with an ongoing theme. A weekly club may be a general crafting club in which a new type of craft is introduced each week. A monthly club may be one in which the same type of craft, such as knitting, is continued during each program. Monthly craft clubs might include jewelry making, paper crafting, scrapbooking, drawing, or learning about various artists or art mediums. To discover the crafts that children in your community might be interested in, develop a Program Interest Survey similar to the one we looked at in chapter 3. This survey will help you plan clubs that children in your community are interested in attending.

Another type of program that works well as an ongoing club involves building with Legos. Building clubs offer children the opportunity to develop or follow plans, expose them to principles of design and engineering, and promote fine motor development.[1] Lego programs can be tied directly to your library's collection and can be planned according to level of difficulty, depending on the age range of participants. Many books supply Lego building plans and information on Lego character collections, and many graphic novels combine

Legos with popular heroes and characters. These books and building-based programs offer a great way to reach reluctant readers who are interested in Lego building. Legos have made their way into several other areas of interest as well, including various video games and robotics, which make great programs for tween patrons.

The traditional book club is another option to consider. For a family-based book club, a chapter book or lengthier picture book can be chosen for families to read together at home, and library program activities can be planned that help support the themes from the book. Book clubs can meet once a month or once a week, depending on the length of the book or the number of books you choose to incorporate. As with any library program, books and book club activities should be developmentally appropriate for the age range of the children who are the focus of your program. Give adult participants a set of guidelines to follow prior to the discussion portion of the program, and ask them to share the guidelines with their children before the first session.[2] For younger children, at-home family activities can be assigned along with hands-on crafts, activities, and games at the library to help children connect to the story in a concrete way. Hands-on activities will help young children identify with the characters and connect children to the plot of the story. Another option is to provide online book club resources for families to complete on their own at home. Examples include links to online activities, questionnaires to complete online, or posts to add to a family book club blog. You may also choose to create a scavenger hunt throughout your community with items or places that reinforce the events in the book. There are many different options for setting up family book clubs. Try a different approach for each book, matching the approach to the theme of the book and the ages of your participants. Book clubs for older children may be marketed for children only, or another option that often works well is an adult-child book club that children attend with an adult of their choice. Book clubs can be offered during times that work for children, for families, or for both, which often means during the evening or on a weekend. Use the survey method to discover which times work best for your community.

Gaming clubs might include electronic games, board games, or card games. Gaming clubs can be offered for young children and families or for older children to attend with their peers. Electronic gaming clubs that focus on computer-based games can meet in your library's computer lab, while gamers who use gaming consoles can meet in your library's program room. You can require participants to bring their own personal handheld devices for programs that involve playing games on personal gaming devices. Programs that incorporate popular card games are appropriate for tweens. Many popular card games include collecting and trading cards, which can be integrated into card gaming programs. Multiple board games can be made available for use during a board game program. Providing many options at the same time makes it fairly easy to offer board games as a program for children of multiple ages and for families.

Storytime and Shared Reading Programs

Most children in kindergarten through second grade still enjoy storytime-style programs during which stories are read to them. Even after children can read for themselves, hearing an adult read aloud continues to help them develop skills that are linked to literacy development. Print motivation skills continue to develop through the early elementary school years, and hearing an adult read aloud helps children develop a love of reading. In addition, auditory, vocabulary, and narrative skills are supported through listening to stories as they are read aloud because children can be exposed to books that they are not ready to read on their own.[3] It is important that your reading programs for children and families promote shared reading as an activity that should be continued at home after the children can read for themselves. In addition to offering family book clubs and storytime-influenced programs, your library can create bibliographies of books that are good for family-shared reading, and book displays can reinforce the books that you choose to add to your book lists.

Outreach Programs

In addition to reaching patrons through programs that are hosted in the library, outreach programs can help you reach elementary school–age children who are unable to get to the library for programs. Outreach might include programs in collaboration with schools, but it also might include programs that take place at various locations after school. Locations where children and families frequently gather are best for successful outreach programming. Locations that often work well for after-school outreach programs include housing authority or neighborhood recreation centers, extended-care programs at schools, laundromats, fast-food restaurants, county health departments, and parks (depending on the time of year).

Outreach programs that are offered through collaborative efforts with schools can provide materials that are not available through the school's library collection. These programs can be especially helpful when several teachers are leading units at the same time, with the public library supplying additional materials for student use. Your library may choose to develop an outreach service that simply delivers books to classrooms—or, depending on the needs of the teacher, you may lead a program for the school or classroom that supports the unit. One popular public library-school collaborative effort is the Lunch Bunch book club.[4] This club meets during the students' lunch hour in their teacher's classroom or in their school library. The school media specialist (or the classroom teacher) and a public librarian facilitate the book discussion while the students eat lunch. If feasible, the public library can supply all the books for the students, or the school library and the public library can split the distribution of books for all participants. The lunchtime book club can be a good motivator for reluctant readers. Availability of staffing and materials at your library will impact the services you are able to provide, but when possible, this type of outreach service can provide value to schools in your library's community.

Your library may also choose to include academic assistance in the form of outreach homework help or reading assistance programs, or both. Many housing and recreational centers offer supplies and space for children to work on homework after school each day. Reaching out to these organizations in your community can help you connect with children whom you may never otherwise see, while also providing a valuable service to the community organizations with which you collaborate. A good place to start is to inquire about the academic help these community organizations might already provide after school and then ask how the library can help. Another option, depending on the age of the children who attend, is to provide a reading-based program in which you simply read a book with the children over several sessions. Reading aloud to children of all ages, as previously mentioned, helps them develop important auditory and literacy skills. Hands-on programs and take-home activities can reinforce the content and themes presented in the book.

When possible, it is important to offer children the opportunity to check out materials during outreach programs, especially during the programs that serve children with limited access to materials. There are a variety of ways you can do this to best fit the capabilities of your library and collection. For example, you might put together book bundles in which a variety of books are checked out together as one item. Books included in these bundles cannot be checked out individually or mixed with other sets. This option works well for libraries with smaller collections because the books that are included in the bundled sets are not taken from the regular collection. Books that are part of a bundled set can be books that have been withdrawn from the collection or paperback books that are purchased in bulk. The point of outreach checkout is to get books into the hands of children who may not otherwise have the opportunity to check out materials from the library. These types of kits do not have to be a great expense in your library's budget. By using books that are inexpensive, withdrawn, or even donated, your library can give children the opportunity to access materials without the concern of replacing expensive items that may not be returned.

Pop-Up Programs

Another method of serving children who may not have the ability to regularly attend library programs is pop-up programming. These types of programs can be outreach programs that are preplanned with schools or other organizations, or they can take place at the library. Pop-up programs are not necessarily announced to participants beforehand, but they can be advertised if preparation of materials depends on an estimated number of participants.

One type of pop-up outreach program is the tabling event, in which a small activity is planned to take place at a table as students arrive at the beginning of school or during lunchtime. A tabling event might include simple games or activities that connect children to services or programs at the library. You may choose to give out various promotional materials for students to take home, such as event calendars or other items with the library's address and hours. This type of outreach program allows you to connect with children and supplies them with information to share with their parents when they go home. Your library may also participate in tabling events that take place during community-wide events for children and families, such as fairs and festivals. By taking the opportunity to engage participants in simple tabling activities, your library can promote upcoming programs while also informing children and families about other library services.

Another type of pop-up program is the passive program. Passive programs usually take place at the library over a period of time. They can be promoted but are not actively led by library staff. Instead, participants are able to take part at their leisure between a beginning and an ending date. Passive programs include such activities as entering a raffle, entering a contest, submitting written reviews of items, or engaging with interactive displays. Passive programs do not require a lot of preparation or upkeep and can be enjoyed by children of various ages and abilities.[5]

STEAM Programs

STEAM programs connect to science, technology, engineering, art, and math. Based on the education movement with the same name, STEAM programs offer the opportunity for libraries to link literacy to science- and math-related concepts. By its very nature, a STEAM program includes hands-on activities, offering participants actual experience with the concepts that are covered in the program. Concepts from STEAM programs can promote informational (nonfiction) books from your library's collection, and the collection, in turn, can support your STEAM programs.[6] STEAM programs for children can be offered as stand-alone programs or as a series of programs.

One type of STEAM-based programming is a maker program or a maker-space. Maker programs involve putting out supplies that children can experiment with to create projects. An alternative to hosting a maker program is to create a makerspace where children can work on their projects over time during visits to the library. This approach requires providing space where projects can be stored between visits. Another way to provide a makerspace for children is to create maker kits. STEAM-related concepts can be supported through hands-on kit activities that offer science, technology, engineering, art, and math experiences. These kits can be placed in plastic containers and made available for children to use while in the library or during outreach programs. Maker kits can be placed at the information desk or in an area near the desk, or they can be organized inside your library's bookmobile or outreach vehicle. If your library offers kits for use in the library, you can require children to check out the kits while they use them. This approach helps keep track of each kit and monitor daily user statistics. Maker kits offer a good alternative for smaller libraries or for libraries that do not have the budget to fund all the supplies and tools needed for full makerspaces.

Community-Wide Book Initiatives

Community-wide book initiatives are a great way to reach out to the entire community as people from many different walks of life all read the same book. Libraries can also create successful community-wide book initiatives specifically for children and families.[7] One way to create such an initiative is to collaborate with area schools in sponsoring a monthlong program based on a mutually chosen book. An author visit at the end of the month can be included as a motivating factor for children who participate in the program. Depending on your library's budget for such programs, your library may cover the author's fees or share the cost with the school or other organizations within the community. Your library also can apply for grants to help cover the costs associated with book purchases, events, and author visits.

Another type of collaborative book project that your library can help sponsor is a Battle of the Books competition.[8] This competition may vary in some ways depending on grade level and community, but the core foundation remains the same. Participants in the Battle read books from a specified list over several months and then compete against other students in the same grades who have read the same books. The contest is usually similar to an academic team quick-recall competition, with teams of students using a buzzer system to answer questions read by a moderator. The Battle of the Books competition works well with tweens and can be developed through a collaboration with your community's schools. Your library may also develop a competition for homeschoolers. The Battle of the Books competition encourages children to read books that they may not otherwise choose to read on their own. Working with schools in your community, your library can help guide the choice of books that are added to the reading lists. Depending on your library's collection budget, you may also be able to support the competition by offering multiple copies of each book for checkout.

Readers' Theater

In addition to book-based initiatives, your library may offer readers' theater programs that provide children the opportunity to perform by reading from a script.[9] Readers' theater allows children to act out stories without having to memorize lines, dress in costume, or even have props (though all those can be an option). Not only does this type of performance allow children to act out stories with a script, but reading from a script also helps children work on important reading skills such as fluency and comprehension. Reading and rereading scripts during practice builds word recognition, narrative skills, and vocabulary. Readers' theater works well with children who have moved past the early stages of reading but are still working on building their skills. The goal of readers' theater is to provide an enjoyable reading experience, which should cultivate a love of reading and, thus, foster print motivation skills.

Reading to Therapy Animals

Programs that engage children in reading to trained therapy animals have become popular at many public libraries. These reading programs can work well for children in a wide range of ages and reading abilities.[10] Public libraries that offer reading programs with therapy animals work with organizations that train animals and their owners to participate in these special programs. Animals are trained to stay calm and listen as children read aloud to them. Children who may struggle with reading aloud are often comforted by the presence of a calm animal who listens without judgment as they read. This type of program allows children to practice reading aloud without being made to feel that their reading abilities are being evaluated by the listener. By helping children develop reading competencies such as fluency and narrative skills in a nonthreatening and relaxed environment, this approach can be very useful with reluctant readers or children with delayed literacy or language skills.

Programs for Homeschool Groups

Although your library may have already developed many collaborative programs with schools in your community, it is important to offer programs for homeschool groups as well, depending on the homeschool population in the community. Many homeschool populations have developed cooperative homeschool groups that meet on specific days. Often, parents of children who attend these groups will serve as instructors in different academic areas. In order to best meet the needs of homeschoolers in your community, it is helpful to reach out to a parent representative of the group. Parent leaders may complete surveys to help determine specific types of programs that homeschoolers may find helpful. Although your library programs will not replace specific content area lessons for homeschool students, you can develop programs that help support specific content areas. For example, you can offer to host a program on a specific historical period, including culture, literature, and hands-on activities. STEAM-based programs may also be offered to help connect homeschool students to specific scientific or mathematical concepts. Programs that teach children about art concepts or specific artists may also be helpful. After you have surveyed the homeschool groups in your community, you may find that many of the programs that you have already developed for school-based and other groups will also work well for homeschool groups.

We have covered many different types of programs in this chapter. This list is by no means exhaustive. There are many programs that you may identify as needed within your library's community that were not mentioned in this chapter. It is important to survey your community and organizations within your community in order to provide the types of programs that are most needed. The next chapter will walk you through each step of program planning, from concept to delivery, including program planning templates for children in kindergarten through second grade and tweens in third through fifth grade.

NOTES

1. Tess Pendergast, "Brick by Brick," *Children and Libraries: The Journal of the Association for Library Service to Children* 10, no. 3 (2012): 20–23.

2. Ginny Moore Kruse, and Kathleen T. Horning, "CCBC Book Discussion Guidelines," Cooperative Children's Book Center, http://ccbc.education.wisc.edu/books/discguide.asp.

3. Derry Koralek, "Reading Aloud with Children of All Ages," Reading Is Fundamental, https://www.naeyc.org/files/yc/file/200303/ReadingAloud.pdf.

4. Jenifer Rank, "Lunch Bunch Book Clubs: A Model Fostering the Love of Reading," *Illinois Reading Council Journal* 41, no. 2 (2013): 22–27.

5. Dana Horrocks, "Passive Programs Throw Down!" Jbrary, https://jbrary.com/passive-programs/.

6. Amy Koester, "Get STEAM Rolling!" *Children and Libraries: The Journal of the Association for Library Service to Children* 12, no. 3 (2014): 22–25.

7. Jane McFann, "'One City, One Book': Creating Community through Reading," *Reading Today* 2, no. 2 (2002): 24.

8. Battle of the Books, "What Is BOB?," http://battleofthebooks.com/what-is-bob/.

9. Tracy D. Garrett, and Dava O'Connor, "Readers' Theater: 'Hold On, Let's Read It Again,'" *Teaching Exceptional Children* 43, no. 1 (2010): 6–13.

10. Susan Black, "Sit, Stay, and Read," *American School Board Journal* 196, no. 12 (2009): 36–37.

Program
Planning

WE HAVE COVERED SEVERAL TYPES OF PROGRAMS FOR
use with children in kindergarten through fifth grade and
the skills that these programs should foster. In this chapter
we will look at each of the specific steps involved in program planning—for various types of programs. The planning process includes
choosing the type of program and the structure it will follow as well as the concepts and subject matter to be addressed, the books and other literacy-based
materials that will be used, and the types of hands-on activities that will be
incorporated. All these choices should be made with the intention of fostering
literacy skills and encouraging children to develop a lifelong love of reading.

Choosing the Type of Program

The first step toward planning your program is to choose the type of program
that will best connect to the audience and the purposes of your program. In
chapter 4, we looked at various types of programs that you might choose to
offer, depending on the age range of your participants. As you consider the type
of program you would like to offer, keep in mind the age and developmental
level of the intended audience. For instance, you probably would not choose
to offer a stand-alone storytime program with puppets and fingerplays to fifth
graders. Such a choice may seem like common sense, but the real point is to
understand the interests, abilities, and developmental levels of participants
and to match activities and content accordingly. The table in figure 5.1 provides guidelines for matching types of programs with grade-level categories.

Although there may be some exceptions (such as making adjustments for
children with special needs or for multigenerational and family programs),

FIGURE 5.1

Types of Programs Suitable for Each Grade Level

PROGRAM TYPES	KINDERGARTEN–SECOND GRADE	THIRD–FIFTH GRADES
Clubs (hobby and interest related)		
Discussion Groups (book clubs)		
Gaming/Technology		
Story-Based		
Author Visit/ Guest Presenter		
Pop-Up/Impromptu		
STEAM (Science, Technology, Engineering, Art, Math)		
Readers' Theater		
Play-Based		
Family/ Multigenerational		
Sensory/ Special Needs		

figure 5.1 provides a quick reference for choosing the types of programs that typically work well with each grade-level group (kindergarten through second grade and third through fifth grade). Notice that several types of programs may be appropriate for both grade categories.

Program Planning Resources

By following a general planning outline for each type of program that you offer, you will make your programs more consistent in quality, timing, and literacy-based activities. Creating a planning outline for your programs also helps in developing a template that can be used for planning future programs of the same type. To help you establish your own program templates and guidelines, program planning outlines are provided at the end of this chapter for each of the program types included in figure 5.1. Lesson plans that are based on specific content, themes, and topics are included in chapter 10. These resources can be used to guide your own program planning practices. Once you have established a system for each type of program, you will find that it becomes easier to shift your plans according to the needs of your participants. Having a flexible plan is always a good practice, no matter the age or needs of the participants.

Another resource you may want to use to help you plan developmentally appropriate programs is your state department of education—particularly the academic standards set by the department. Although you may not be planning classroom lessons that need to follow these standards, they can help guide your programming choices. Referring to your state's academic (or Common Core) standards can help you understand what children are expected to learn during specific grades in school.[1] Being familiar with your state's standards can help you tailor your programs to be developmentally appropriate for most of the children who attend. Again, there are always some exceptions, so remember to be flexible and follow the needs and abilities of your participants, but also use these standards to connect to concepts that are most likely to be of interest to your target grade and age levels.

In addition to incorporating state academic standards, you will want to plan activities that foster the reading skills and the five modes of multiliteracy that we covered in chapter 2. When choosing books for your program, remember to be intentional about choosing books that encourage decoding, comprehension, and fluency skills for beginning readers. Choose materials for intermediate readers that provide an opportunity to build thinking and reasoning skills. For all levels of readers, remember to build in activities that encourage social interaction and language development as well as opportunities for hands-on learning and exploration. Choosing program concepts, activities, and books that support one another will create an atmosphere in which children are learning and having fun.

Concepts, Themes, and Topics

After or in conjunction with selecting the type of program you will offer, you will want to choose the concepts and topics on which you will build your program. Using state academic standards is one strategy for making these choices, and there are other strategies that can help you plan programs that will be of interest to your potential participants. Use the lesson plans in chapter 10 to get you started, and look at the programs that other libraries are offering. You may discover some program ideas that could also be successful at your library.

The Association for Library Service to Children (ALSC) is another resource for programming guidance. ALSC offers programming information through conferences, continuing education, and online resources (www.ala.org/alsc/). One resource available on the ALSC website that is particularly helpful for program planning is a list of programming ideas to use with school-age kids.[2] This list includes book-related activities, community services programs, craft programs, drama and performance-related programs, gaming programs, and more. Suggestions for programs involving community guests are also included on this list, providing a starting point for brainstorming the possibilities that exist within your own community.

As you consider themes for your programs, it is important to do research on the trends and interests among the children in your community. In addition to developing ongoing communication with regular patrons, you can gather information about program interests by asking patrons and potential program participants to complete simple surveys. These surveys can be completed in person through paper surveys or made available to participants online. Parents can be asked to help younger children complete the surveys, and upper elementary school-age children can complete surveys on their own. You may also choose to offer a passive program in which older children can submit ideas for programs. The Program Interest Survey template in the appendix can be modified to meet the specific needs of your library. Use this template as a guideline or reproduce it in its entirety for creating surveys for your own program planning.

Schools in your community may also help you discover the types of programs that are likely to receive the most interest. Ask school administrators and teachers if you can distribute surveys to parents and students to better serve the needs of the community. Teachers may also be willing to complete interest surveys in order to help guide community programs. You may want to explore the possibility of establishing a collaborative partnership with schools to create clubs or to cosponsor programs or book clubs at schools. By connecting on a personal level with students at schools, you can gather information about interests through conversations with students and promote library programs during your programs at schools. Working directly with schools can provide valuable information to help build programs that are most needed in your community.

Program Structure and Scheduling

After you choose the concept, theme, and topics for your program, you will want to consider the overall structure. This process includes determining the sequence that your program will follow—in other words, how much time you will allot for each part of your program and in what order you will present the parts. You will want to consider the ages and abilities of potential participants as you plan the amount of time you will spend for each part of your program. It is also a good rule of thumb to alternate between active and passive engagement in order to maintain the interest and attention of your participants. Younger children, in particular, need the alternation between moving and listening. This strategy helps build in natural transitions between each part of your program—a feature that is needed by young children.

In addition to planning the structure of individual programs, you will want to consider whether the content is more appropriate for a single program or for multiple sessions. If your program will work best across several sessions, you will need to decide how many will be most appropriate. For example, it is common for story-based programs to include four to six sessions; however, club-based programs are often ongoing or seasonal. Figure 5.2 provides guidelines to help you choose the number of sessions that are most appropriate for each type of program. Remember to balance the difficulty level and the developmental abilities of your participants, and be aware of seasonal or holiday schedules that may impact programs that are spread out over several weeks.

In addition to planning the individual program schedule and the number of sessions to be offered for each program, you will want to consider the day, time, and exact date when your program will be best received. Several approaches will help you make each of these decisions. First, it is important to be familiar with the events that take place in your community. Although it may not be possible to avoid scheduling your program at the same time as another popular event, being aware of other community events can help you limit the number of times that such a conflict occurs, thereby maximizing the number of people who may be able to attend your program.

FIGURE 5.2

Number of Program Sessions for Each Grade Level

PROGRAM TYPES	KINDERGARTEN–SECOND GRADE	THIRD–FIFTH GRADES
Clubs (hobby and interest related)	Ongoing/Seasonal	Ongoing/Seasonal
Discussion Groups (book clubs)		4–6 sessions per book
Gaming/Technology		Ongoing/Seasonal
Story-Based	4–6 sessions per season	
Author Visit/ Guest Presenter	1 session or 4–6 sessions leading to visit	1 session or 4–6 sessions leading to visit
Pop-Up/Impromptu	1 session or ongoing	1 session or ongoing
STEAM (Science, Technology, Engineering, Art, Math)	1 session or 4–6 sessions	1 session or 4–6 sessions
Readers' Theater		4–6 weeks of practice; 1 final performance
Play-Based	1 session or 4–6 sessions	
Family/ Multigenerational	1 session or 4–6 sessions	1 session or 4–6 sessions
Sensory/ Special Needs	1 session or 4–6 sessions	1 session or 4–6 sessions

One way to make sure that you are aware of other events is to attend community council and early childhood council meetings. These groups may be known by different names in your community, but, essentially, they are community groups with open membership for community members with the same interests. Council members share information about the services and programs they provide and are able to network with other members of the council. You may also discover opportunities for building collaborative partnerships as you share information about library programs and learn more about the services and programs provided by other members of the council.

Another way to make sure that you are aware of other community events is through working with your community's department of tourism and chamber of commerce. Community tourism departments often publish community calendars and newsletters with information about local events. Not only will this information from the department of tourism and chamber of commerce help you stay informed about other activities within your community, but you can also share information about library programs with other organizations through the same means. Other places to find and share event information are your local media outlets, including the newspaper, radio stations, and television stations. By staying up-to-date on community events and sharing information about library events, you will increase the likelihood of creating a successful program.

Second, collaborative partnerships with schools will help you stay informed about school-sponsored activities that are scheduled. Again, it is not always possible to avoid overlap between library and school events, but it is helpful to be aware of school event schedules as you plan your library programs. Knowing what extracurricular activities are lacking at schools can also help you discover program areas where the library might help fill a need. In order to be sure that these areas are actually of interest, it is important that you communicate with teachers or other representatives from the school and, if possible, distribute interest surveys at school. There may be interest in extracurricular activities for which the school does not have room in the schedule. The library can help fill this void by working with the school to plan and provide programs, perhaps in the form of an outreach program hosted at the school or other community venue or offered at the library for students from multiple schools from across the community. It is particularly important to align the schedule of programs such as this with school-sponsored activities in order to best serve the needs of potential participants and to maximize the number of participants who are able to attend.

Program Materials and Activities

After choosing the type of program you will offer, the concepts and themes you will include, and the overall structure of the program, you are ready to select program materials and hands-on activities that you will use in your program.

BOOKS AND OTHER LITERACY-BASED MATERIALS

With literacy at the heart of library programming, choosing quality books for program use is crucial. For story-based programs, you may choose books before you plan your activities, or you may choose your concept and theme first and then choose books and activities to support your theme. For book discussion groups and readers' theater, it is a good idea to choose a book prior to your program and then base program activities on the book you have chosen. The order in which you plan and choose materials should be determined by the type of program and the age of your program's intended audience.

When choosing a book (or books) as the first step in program planning, you will want to consider the literacy and reading skills that are fostered by the text. By choosing books that help foster such skills as vocabulary, decoding, fluency, and comprehension, you are more likely to make intentional programming choices that make the biggest impact on your program participants. For example, when choosing books for story-based programs for children in kindergarten through second grade, keep shared reading in mind. This approach means choosing books with rich vocabulary, opportunities for conversation, and a captivating message. It also means choosing books with illustrations that capture and accurately convey the events in the text of the story. Most children in kindergarten through second grade will still enjoy being read to in programs, and books for this age range may include picture books. Themes for story-based programs are often chosen before the books and activities. This practice can work well for programs that connect to specific areas of interest, specific genres, or specific literacy skills. Themes, however, can pose a problem if your practice is more about choosing a book simply because it fits a theme rather than choosing a book based on its merit or literacy value. Consider your practice as you decide whether you will plan the theme first or choose books and materials first for programs for children in kindergarten through second grade. Remember that intentionality is best practice when choosing the books that you will use in your programs.

When you choose books for programs for third through fifth graders, keep in mind that these books will be used mainly for independent reading outside the program. Although you may read portions of these books aloud as a group, it is most likely that participants in third through fifth grade will read most of the books on their own. For example, books that are chosen for book-discussion programs are read by participants before the program, as are books connected to author visit programs. Books for these types of programs for children in third through fifth grade will usually be chosen first, with support activities planned after the books are chosen. In these types of programs, the theme of the program is the book itself, though activities that highlight themes in the book should be planned as part of the program.

Similarly, when you plan a readers' theater program, the book will be the first thing that you choose, with supporting activities planned next. Readers' theater scripts are often adapted from the original book. Scripts can be adapted by library staff, or you may choose to follow the original text of an entire book, if the length and vocabulary fit your needs. A lengthy picture book often makes a good choice for a readers' theater program for third through fifth graders. When you choose a book for readers' theater, it is important to consider the age and reading abilities of each program participant. Although you likely will choose the book for your performance first, you will need to make adjustments to the script based on the reading abilities of your participants once the program starts. It is important to build in practice sessions before the performance. After you have planned and scheduled your readers' theater program sessions and participants have registered for the program, a good way to start the first session is to introduce participants to the original text of the book. As the group practices reading the text aloud, you will get a feel for the levels and abilities that are represented within the group. The next step is to make adaptations to the text as you create a script that each of your participants is able to read aloud successfully through practice. Readers' theater offers a great opportunity for participants to practice reading aloud and provides children the opportunity to perform without having to memorize lines.

Whether you choose books for your program based on a chosen theme or you choose a theme based on concepts from one of your chosen books, the next step is to plan activities for your program.

HANDS-ON ACTIVITIES

Program activities should engage participants in hands-on interaction with the concepts, skills, and themes that are presented through the books used in your program. Whether you choose books or a theme first, the activities that you plan should support the overall intent of your program, with literacy as the central focus. When participants are engaged in physically manipulating materials that are representative of the content that they have read, real-world applications and learning experiences bring the text to life.

Craft projects work well as part of a literacy-based program with most children in kindergarten through second grade. Crafting in programs can offer children the opportunity to physically manipulate materials that are linked to the content and themes represented within program books and materials. This physical manipulation of materials can expand comprehension skills because children are connecting with the story on a tangible level.[3] As with other activities, crafts should be developmentally appropriate and fall within the interest levels of your intended audience. Materials should be safe for the ages that are represented in your program, and instructions should be written or given in a way that is easily understood by your program participants.

Crafts can have the same hands-on value for tweens in the third through fifth grades. Just as with participants in kindergarten through second grade, it is important to offer crafts that are developmentally appropriate for tweens. Crafts can be used to expand on concepts represented in your program's book of focus. Crafts can be ongoing over several sessions, or they can change with each session in programs that take place over several sessions. Crafts can also be used to facilitate discussion between participants during a book discussion program. When tweens are engaged in a hands-on project, such as a craft, the project can serve as a stepping-off point for conversation and interaction. Written instructions can also link participants to literacy skill and conversation skill development when participants collaborate on a craft project that is connected to the program's book(s). Crafts can provide encouragement for language and literacy skills as well as social and fine motor skills among participants of all ages.

Gaming is another type of activity that can be of value to literacy-based programs for children. Gaming might include board games, social games, or technology-based games. Incorporating interactive games into your programs can provide a connection to literacy and learning.[4] Games also help children learn rules and strategic thinking as well as social skills, such as turn-taking, self-control, and patience. Games can connect to the various modes of multiliteracy, as well. Although video games obviously connect to digital media and social literacies, they also foster visual and textual literacy. Board games can also foster these same literacy skills. When games are used to support the content and themes of books in a program, they serve much the same purpose as crafts. Hands-on engagement with games that are connected to the books used in programs can help children process and comprehend the content that they read.

Other play-based activities, such as dramatic play for younger children and readers' theater and acting for tweens, can provide hands-on engagement opportunities that reinforce the content from the book(s) and other activities included in the program. Play can be used to expand or revisit themes and ideas from reading, which helps make the content more meaningful. Puppet play can help younger children develop narrative and sequencing skills by inviting the children to retell a story that was read aloud to them in their own words and from their own memories. This type of play-based activity leads to growth toward comprehension skills that children develop as they become more advanced readers.

Discussion-based activities are the largest part of book discussion group programs, which are most appropriate with children in the third through fifth grades. This segment of the program encourages participants to discuss a specific section of the book that they were encouraged to read independently prior to the scheduled program. Discussion-based activities encourage language, social, reasoning, and memory skill development and require comprehension skills for participants to contribute to the group discussion. Discussion-based activities that are a part of book groups require that readers have developed intermediate skills, including metacognition and executive functioning skills, in order to contribute thoughts and opinions to the discussion.

Discussion-based activities can be introduced to children in kindergarten through second grade through such practices as interactive reading. In this type of reading, children are encouraged to share their thoughts in response to open-ended questions asked by the reader. These questions usually relate to events as they are happening within the story or elicit the child's prediction of what will happen next in the story. Other discussion-based activities can be offered at interactive stations during story-based programs. Adults should be encouraged to interact with children at various stations that include activities that stimulate conversation and other social skills.

We have covered several areas of planning for children's programs, including choosing program type, developing program outlines, selecting program concepts and themes, establishing program structure and scheduling, choosing materials, and planning activities. You will find program planning outlines for various types of programs over the next few pages. These outlines can be used to help you plan each part of your program. Simply use the outline as a template to help guide each of the areas you will include. Remember that the outlines are offered as guidelines. It is important to keep your plans flexible and to make plans based on the needs of your community and program participants.

NOTES

1. Common Core State Standards Initiative, "Standards in Your State," www.core standards.org/standards-in-your-state/.

2. Association for Library Service to Children, "Programs for School-Aged Kids," www.ala.org/alsc/kickstart.

3. Kathryn Hatter, "What Are the Benefits of Arts and Crafts for Children?" www.livestrong.com/article/80368-benefits-arts-crafts-children/.

4. Ron T. Brown and Tamara Kasper, "The Fusion of Literacy and Games: A Case Study in Assessing the Goals of a Library Video Game Program," http://hdl.handle .net/2142/46053.

Clubs
(Hobby and Interest-Related)

Before the Program

CHOOSE THE CLUB THEME Decide on the overall theme of your club-based program. Decide whether your program will consist of several types of activities or concentrate on one craft or hobby-related activity. Choose a theme that is of interest to your participants and is developmentally appropriate for their age. Decide how many sessions you will offer and the structure that each session will follow.

CHOOSE PREREGISTRATION OR DROP-IN For programs that require supplies for each participant, or if your work space or program is small, it is best to ask participants to preregister. Knowing the number of participants ahead of time will help you ensure that enough space and supplies are available for those who attend. If you have plenty of supplies on hand or a larger space, or both, you may choose to offer your program as a drop-in activity for which preregistration is not required. Drop-in programs are typically offered open-house style, and participants arrive and depart at their own discretion during a given time span. When offering club-based programs with several sessions that require preregistration, you may choose either to require registration for each session or to permit participants to register for the entire set of sessions. You will want to consider the level of interest and the best way to serve your potential participants.

PLAN THE NUMBER OF PARTICIPANTS If your program will require registration, decide on the total number of participants that your program can accommodate. For programs with more difficult activities or programs that will require more one-on-one interaction between the leader and participants, it is best to set a lower number.

CHOOSE BOOKS Choose books that you will read during your program or that participants should read in order to participate in the club.

Choose display books that are connected to the subject of your program, and place the books in a convenient location where participants will most likely see them and consider checking them out at the close of the program.

CHOOSE ACTIVITIES Choose hands-on activities that support your theme, and encourage your participants to interact with the concepts presented by the books that you have chosen to use as part of your program. The number of activities you choose should be based on the amount of time you will offer for participation in the program.

PREPARE ACTIVITY MATERIALS Prepare the materials that will be needed by participants. Preparation might include purchasing, printing, coloring, or precutting items. Any tools that participants will need should also be pre-chosen and prepared. Materials and tools should be placed on trays or in baskets and made easily accessible for participants. For multi-session programs, it is important to take inventory after each session to be sure that you will have adequate supplies that are in working order for the next session.

PREPARE INSTRUCTION TABLE TENTS Create table tents with instructions for each interactive station. Instructions on table tents should be in simple language and written in the fewest words possible. If an activity requires lengthier instructions, use the table tent as a station label and place printed instruction sheets on the table.

During the Program

WELCOME Plan an introduction to your program. Briefly introduce the topic of your program and any upcoming sessions of the club. Explain the structure of the program and how each session will work.

INTRODUCE ACTIVITIES Introduce any whole-group activities that you have planned first, and offer any stations or independent activities during the second half of your program. This way, participants will be introduced to concepts together and then be able to apply those concepts to hands-on activities. Introduce the activities that you will be offering. Before beginning program activities, provide any special instructions that participants will need.

PROGRAM ACTIVITIES Encourage participants to engage with program concepts through hands-on activities. For multigenerational programs, encourage interaction between adults and children. For programs that are intended for children only, offer activities that encourage interaction between participants. Table tents and instructions should be placed at activity stations as needed.

Closing the Program

PREPARE PARTICIPANTS As the program approaches the scheduled ending time, announce how much time remains before participants must gather their supplies and clean up. Distribute information about the next session or about upcoming programs that may be of interest to participants.

Discussion Groups
for Third through Fifth Grade

Before the Program

CHOOSE THE BOOK(S) For a book discussion group for tweens, you will want to choose a book that will draw the most interest. Before choosing a book, consider distributing an interest survey or choose a book that might be a part of a school reading competition, such as Battle of the Books. Make books available for pickup or checkout before the first program so that participants will have enough time to read the assigned amount of the book. Exactly when you make books available will depend on how many chapters you ask participants to read before the first program. Allow enough time to ensure that most participants have read the same amount of the book and will be ready to discuss the assigned chapters.

PLAN THE PROGRAM STRUCTURE The structure of the program should be determined by the type of discussion group you choose to offer. If your program will be for tweens without adults, you will want to facilitate discussion through interactive activities. Combining discussion with social activities will help break the ice and draw participants into the conversation in a natural way. If your program is intended for tweens and adults, it is helpful to preplan discussion questions and interactive games that will encourage interaction among the entire group as well as some individual activities that will encourage interaction between tweens and their adult partners.

PLAN THE NUMBER OF PARTICIPANTS The number of potential participants will be determined by the type of discussion group you choose to offer as well as the size of your space. Multi-session programs that are intended for tweens to attend without adults will not require as much space as programs intended for tweens and adults, so your maximum number for tween and adult programs may be lower than the number for tweens alone.

PLAN DISCUSSION QUESTIONS AND OTHER ACTIVITIES When planning discussion questions, it is important to connect to the content and themes of the book by selecting developmentally appropriate discussion questions and activities. Questions should be open-ended, encouraging participants to develop thoughtful answers rather than simple yes or no answers. Whole-group activities can be used to support questions and help participants arrive at the answers.

PREPARE PROGRAM MATERIALS It is helpful to create name tags prior to each session of your program to help participants get to know one another and to help you learn the names of your participants. You may also choose to offer refreshments depending on the time of day and number of participants. In addition to refreshments, you will want to prepare any materials that may be needed for hands-on activities, such as materials for interactive games or crafts that expand on the concepts and themes of the book.

During the Program

WELCOME At the beginning of the first session of your program, describe the structure of the program and how the discussion will work. Distribute a list of chapters and upcoming dates. Ask participants to introduce themselves to the group.

INTRODUCE DISCUSSION Emphasize the importance of reading according to the outlined schedule so that all participants will be able to discuss the same material at the same time. Emphasize the importance of not reading ahead so as not to divulge any of the plot to anyone who has not yet read future chapters.

INTRODUCE ACTIVITIES After the group discussion portion of the program, introduce hands-on activities. These might include interactive or technology-based games, crafts, or other activities that reinforce concepts from the book. You may offer one interactive station or several stations, depending on the content that you would like to highlight from the reading.

Closing the Program

PREPARE PARTICIPANTS As the program approaches the scheduled ending time, announce how much time remains before participants must gather their supplies and clean up. Distribute information about the next session or about upcoming programs that may be of interest to participants.

Gaming and Technology
for Third through Fifth Grade

Before the Program

CHOOSE THE GAME(S) Consider games that align with the interests of your potential participants. This step includes choosing the game format and gaming systems that you will provide. Computer-based programs can be offered in your library's computer lab, if available. If your library does not have a computer screen or the capability to project games onto a screen, consider offering a gaming session in which participants bring their own devices. Sandbox Interactive games can be accessed by personal devices, and individuals can participate on their own or with others in the program. It is important to find out what games and gaming systems are of the most interest to tweens in your community and investigate what you need to do in order to facilitate a gaming program. Ask your library's IT department to help facilitate the program if you are not familiar with the required technology.

PLAN THE NUMBER OF PARTICIPANTS The number of participants will be determined by the space and the number of devices that your library has available for use. For gaming programs in which participants bring their own devices, consider the amount of assistance that might be needed in order to set your maximum number. Consider having a waiting list as part of your registration in order to serve the most patrons. This list will also help you track the level of interest in case your library is able to add sessions in the future.

PREPARE SUPPLIES For programs that require library-owned devices, it is important to have all devices set up and ready for play prior to the program. Preregistration is crucial in order to make sure that you have an adequate number of devices for all participants. For programs that require your library's computer lab, make sure that computers are able to access games (if played online) and that all applications are updated. If participants will be using their own devices, it is important to test Wi-Fi connections and to make sure that participants will be able to access all required online components of the game.

CHOOSE SUPPORT ACTIVITIES Hands-on crafting activities can be used to support the content of some popular technology-based games. In addition, there are many informational texts about popular games and game design that may be of interest to program participants. Consider making these texts available for program participants, either for use during the program or for checkout afterward, or both.

During the Program

WELCOME Welcome participants to the program and give brief instructions at the door. If more in-depth instructions need to be given, ask participants to come in and wait until all participants have arrived. Have a printed list of registrants handy to ensure that patrons who are preregistered are admitted to the program. This list also helps in the event that you have patrons from the waiting list who are expecting to be admitted. In the event that not everyone on the preregistration list comes to the program, you may want to use the waiting list to fill spaces in the order in which the names appear on the list.

INTRODUCE RULES AND PROCEDURES Announce any rules before beginning the gaming process. If participants will need to take turns with a device, be sure to have a system in place for timing. Some games will have more specific rules that you may want to review at this time. It is important to give this information prior to the beginning of the gaming process.

PROMOTE PARTICIPATION Tween participants in gaming programs may need to be reminded periodically of the rules as well as guided through any turn-taking requirements. Participants may also have questions about how to navigate through the game. If you are not proficient in the features of the game and how to navigate through it, encourage participants to help one another. In addition, consider having informational texts handy because they might help you answer questions.

Closing the Program

PREPARE PARTICIPANTS In a gaming program for tweens, it is especially helpful to announce throughout the program how much time remains. Tweens often get lost in the game and are not aware of time passing. Keeping track of the time will help ensure that participants have adequate time to come to a good stopping place before the end of the program. Consider distributing information about upcoming programs as well as surveys for future gaming program interests. Such surveys will help you plan future gaming programs that connect to the interests of your participants.

Story-Based Program
for Kindergarten through Second Grade

Before the Program

CHOOSE BOOKS AND LITERACY-BASED MATERIALS Consider books that foster literacy-based skills. If your program has a theme or a specific target subject, remember that skill cultivation is more important than connection to the theme; however, books may be chosen that do both. Choose other materials (such as visual aids, technology-based materials, and sensory-based materials) that encourage the development of multi-literacy skills. Incorporate printed text as much as possible, and invite children to help read print aloud as you move through the program.

CHOOSE PROGRAM CONCEPTS, THEMES, AND TOPICS Concepts, themes, and topics should connect to the interests and literacy skill developmental levels of your participants. If you choose a program theme prior to selecting books and literacy-based materials, be sure to seek books that not only fit within your chosen theme but also connect to multiliteracy skill development. Consider surveying children, families, and schools in your community to identify areas of interest as well as areas of need. This information can help you choose themes and concepts that will be of the most value to your community.

CHOOSE PROGRAM STRUCTURE AND SCHEDULING Most children in kindergarten through second grade enjoy story-based programs that include hands-on activities, crafts, and interactive stations. Programs for this age range should last about one hour, with the first half of the program dedicated to whole-group reading and literacy-based activities and the second half devoted to hands-on activities.

CHOOSE GROUP ACTIVITIES Choose activities that connect to the concepts and skills that are represented by the books and literacy-based materials that you use during the whole-group portion of your program. Activities might include social games, music and movement experiences, or reading simple text aloud. Puppets and visual aids may also be used as supportive tools during whole-group activities with children in kindergarten through second grade.

CHOOSE INTERACTIVE ACTIVITIES Hands-on activities should be offered at individual stations throughout the program area. Programs that are intended for adults and children together should include activity stations that encourage interaction between adults and children. Interactive stations during programs for children without adults should encourage interaction between participants. Consider activities that connect to your themes and the literacy skills that are a part of your program focus. It is important to choose activities that focus on the process or the experience rather than the finished product. For this reason, include instructions (in text with minimal pictures as needed) rather than provide completed examples. Some children this age will strive to replicate an example rather than engage with the materials in a way that helps them learn from the experience. A good rule of thumb is to limit the number of interactive stations to four or five. Too many choices may overwhelm some children.

During the Program

WELCOME Take a moment to introduce yourself and briefly explain the format of the program. Explain that the first half of the program will include whole-group activities and that interactive stations will be available during the second half. If your program includes adults, explain that it is important for them to also participate by interacting with their child during the program.

OPENING ACTIVITY Choose an icebreaker activity that introduces children to one another and to the concepts that you will address through your chosen books and stories. This activity should be fun with low-pressure expectations in order to encourage participation.

OPENING BOOK Choose an opening book or story that will help introduce the overall theme or content of your program. Choose a book that is developmentally appropriate with an appropriate amount of text on each page for the age of your audience. The text of the book should be supported by the illustrations, and unfamiliar words should be explained as you go. As you read, be sure to ask open-ended questions, such as "What might happen next?" or "What choices might the characters make?" Your chosen book should support literacy skill development and comprehension.

WHOLE-GROUP INTERACTIVE ACTIVITY Use a hands-on activity to connect participants to the theme of your program. Interactive activities might include group games, activities that engage children in retelling or sequencing of details of the story, or a reenactment of the story with props.

STORYTELLING/PRESENTATION Engage students through a storytelling or readers' theater performance of a related story. You may want to use puppets, props, or storytelling magnet board pieces to support parts of the story.

INDIVIDUAL INTERACTIVE ACTIVITIES Choose four to five interactive stations for children (and adults, if present) to complete. These stations should connect directly to the stories and group activities you choose for the program, reemphasizing lessons learned or important details of the stories. Interactive activities should provide hands-on opportunities for learning. You may want to look at the Common Core and academic standards for your state, your school system, or both, and connect the activities to the standards. Linking your program activities to the standards also provides an opportunity for collaborative outreach to kindergarten through second-grade teachers in your community.

Closing the Program

PREPARE PARTICIPANTS As participants work at the interactive stations, announce the time that remains before the end of the program (at fifteen, ten, and five minutes). These reminders will help participants prepare for the transition and manage their time as they complete each of the activity stations. At the close of the program, meet participants at the door and distribute information about upcoming programs.

Author Visits and Guest Presenters

Before the Program

CHOOSE THE PROGRAM Programs that feature children's authors and guest presenters can be used with children in kindergarten through second grade and with tweens in third through fifth grade. These programs can be sponsored solely by your library or as collaborative projects with schools or the entire community. When choosing authors or guest presenters for a program, it is important to reach out to the community to survey interest among potential participants. If the author or guest is particularly well-known, schools and other community organizations may be interested in cosponsoring the program with your library. As you choose authors, consider the interests of children and schools within your community. Look at the Common Core or academic standards for your state. Contact teachers and ask what authors and books are included in their curriculum. Contact school library media specialists and ask if they are interested in collaborating to plan author visits. If the answer is yes, ask for their thoughts on possible authors. Consider your budget and make contacts with publishers and agents of possible authors. Consider the type of guest presenter that you would like to include in a program. Base your choices on the needs and interests of the community. Reach out to the community through surveys and conversations with organizations and schools, and gather information to help you as you plan programs that feature a guest presenter. You might want to consider hosting a program with a guest presenter from your community, thereby supporting local individuals and organizations. For nonlocal guest presenters, consider your budget and research the types of presenters you wish to host. Contact guest presenters about fees prior to inviting them to present at a program. Many state library systems provide a guest presenter list on their website. This list often includes information on fees and reviews written by library staff in your state who have worked with the presenters.

PLAN THE NUMBER OF PARTICIPANTS Community-wide, collaborative programs that feature authors or guest presenters can be planned in multiple parts to accommodate the largest number of your target audience. The venue for each program session will impact the number of people you can accommodate, and presenters may have preferences regarding crowd size as well. As you plan each individual program, be sure to take into account the locations and venues where your program will take place. If your program will take place at one of the community's schools, you will know exactly how many participants will fit in the space; however, if you will host programs for schools at the library, it is important to inquire how many students might be in attendance in order to make plans accordingly.

PREPARE ACTIVITY MATERIALS Authors and guest presenters may bring their own materials; however, they may also request that you prepare specific items in advance. If you are collaborating with a school or other organization, the preparations can be divided with the cosponsoring agency. It is important to stay in contact with authors and guest presenters and make sure you have prepared any materials that are needed. Visit schools and distribute information about the authors and guest presenters in order to make sure that students are aware of the upcoming program. If your budget allows, provide books written by visiting authors prior to the program. Funds can often be secured through grants or by working with schools, other literacy-based services in the community, and your Friends of the Library group.

During the Program

AUTHOR VISIT

Introduce the author: Visiting schools and distributing books written by the author help ensure that students are aware of and are reading books by the author. Teachers may be able to integrate books by the author into their curriculum, which helps introduce students to the work of the author prior to the author's visit.

Program activities: Author visits can be one-day programs, or activities can be spread over many days or weeks, depending on the target age and length of books that children read as part of the visit. Program sessions can include in-school book clubs, discussions at the library, community-wide discussions, meet-and-greet sessions with the author, or any combination of these.

GUEST PRESENTER

Introduce the presenter: Concepts that are linked to the guest presenter can be introduced through several smaller programs prior to the larger program with the guest presenter. These mini sessions can take place throughout the community, at the library, or at schools and can help promote the guest speaker's presentation. Book displays at the library can also help promote upcoming programs.

Program activities: Mini programs prior to the presentation can be hosted at the library with hands-on activities for participants. Other programs can also be presented throughout the community with content that supports the guest presenter's material.

After the Program

REVISIT THE PROGRAM After the guest presenter or author has spoken, extension programs can be planned. Other books written by the same author may be used as classroom extensions at school, or continuing book clubs may be hosted at the library. Additional programs that allow children to experience activities similar to those presented by a guest can help connect children with the content. Future visits may be planned with the same author or guest presenter—or other guests who present similar content.

Pop-Up or Impromptu Program

Before the Program

CHOOSE ACTIVITIES Choose activities that can be easily completed by participants in just a few seconds. Choose activities that are developmentally appropriate for the age or grade level of the participant. For children in kindergarten through second grade, pop-up programs may include impromptu story-based programs or hands-on, experience-based activities. Although a pop-up program will seem spontaneous to patrons, planning and preparing the materials, as well as the way you will track participation, should be completed prior to launching the program. Planning a pop-up program enables you to intentionally connect with literacy skills through simple activities that participants can complete as they visit the library. Pop-up program activities for tweens in third through fifth grade may include activities such as answering questions to enter a drawing, choosing a book from a basket of books, or writing a brief statement.

PREPARE ACTIVITY MATERIALS Materials for pop-up programs should be prepared prior to launching the program, but this step should not be time consuming because the activities are simple. Paper slips or craft sticks can be used for drawing names. Pieces of lined paper and pencils can be supplied for writing or drawing activities. For pop-up story-based programs, books can be preselected and then participants can choose which book to read from the stack.

During the Program

ENCOURAGE PARTICIPATION Patrons can be invited to participate as they visit the library, or a message can be posted through social media announcing the program the day that it begins. You may choose to reward participants in some simple way, such as by drawing a name for a prize or by distributing promotional items such as pencils or other library marketing items. You might consider connecting your pop-up program to assignments at community schools through collaborating with teachers. Teachers may be willing to give class credit or other awards at school for participation.

Closing the Program

COLLECT INFORMATION If your pop-up program takes place over several days, be sure to post information and reminders about when the program will end. Use impromptu project completion to collect information such as the times of day and days of the week that most patrons of a certain age and grade level visit the library, the age and grade level of participants, the number of patrons interested in specific books or content, or the areas in which you might build more programming content.

STEAM Program
(Science, Technology, Engineering, Art, Math)

Before the Program

CHOOSE ACTIVITIES Activities for STEAM programs should be interactive and offer children the opportunity to experiment and make discoveries. Choose science activities that are challenging but also developmentally appropriate and of interest to your target age group. Science programs are often messy, so make sure your activities are offered in a suitable space that is easy to clean up. Choose STEAM technology-based programs that differ from your regular technology or gaming programs. Technology-based STEAM programs can connect to other areas of interest, such as science or art, to engage children in hands-on manipulation of real-world objects. Engineering activities may be as simple as building with Lego blocks or marshmallows and toothpicks. Choose engineering activities that can be connected to objects and places that children in your program see in their own community. Art activities can include crafts, or you may choose to focus on connecting children with artwork and artists and the techniques they used. Choose activities that expose participants to art techniques through hands-on experiments and opportunities to create art on their own. Math activities, when coupled with other areas such as science or technology, can introduce children to math concepts in a fun way. Encourage children to use their mathematical reasoning skills through projects that involve hands-on experiments and observation activities.

PLAN THE NUMBER OF PARTICIPANTS As you set the number of participants for your STEAM program, consider the ages and abilities of the participants and the level of difficulty of the activities. STEAM programs that require a lot of supplies and guidance should have a small number of participants.

PREPARE ACTIVITY MATERIALS Materials and supplies should be prepared prior to the program. Because of the interactive nature of STEAM-based activities, requiring preregistration can help you know the number of participants that will need supplies. Always prepare a few extra supplies to be safe. Provide guidance or prepare table tents with instructions at activity stations if participants are expected to follow specific procedures during any of your program activities.

During the Program

WELCOME Welcome participants and invite them to take a seat. Give instructions or information about the structure of the program. If you will have a whole-group activity prior to individual activities, provide information about how the schedule will work. Give participants information before they begin doing any activities, and explain the importance of the information portion of your program.

INTRODUCE CONCEPTS Concepts can be introduced during the informational portion of your program. Concepts should include vocabulary and procedures associated with the activities you will offer. Encourage participants to ask questions and share their ideas and thoughts about the concepts that are a part of your program. STEAM programs are naturally interactive, and it is important for participants to have a clear understanding of concepts in order to engage with the supplies that are included in the hands-on portion of your program.

PROGRAM ACTIVITIES Choose STEAM-based program activities that foster reasoning skills, creative thinking, and vocabulary skills and that expose participants to each of the multiliteracy skill areas. Choose activities that are linked to at least one STEAM area (science, technology, engineering, art, or math), and promote hands-on experimental engagement through manipulation of the supplies that you provide.

Closing the Program

PREPARE PARTICIPANTS It is especially important to announce how much time remains in a STEAM-based program because experimental activities can take longer for participants to complete. Give a countdown of the time that remains as you approach the end of the program, and encourage participants to clean their area and gather any projects that they will need to take home. Provide handouts about any experiments or activities that participants want to try at home, along with information about upcoming STEAM-based programs.

Readers' Theater
for Third through Fifth Grade

Before the Program

CHOOSE THE BOOK A good readers' theater book will include dialogue between several characters. Participants can read from the book, or you may choose to adapt the book into a script. Books with humor translate well as readers' theater productions, and simple props or costumes can help communicate the story to the audience. Picture books with vivid illustrations can help you choose props, backdrops, and costumes. Choose a book with easy-to-understand language and vocabulary that is familiar to your target participants.

PLAN THE NUMBER OF PARTICIPANTS The number of readers you will have will depend on the number of characters that are in the story that you choose. You may also choose to add nonspeaking parts or assign other roles to program participants, such as prop designer, costume designer, or other backstage support. Ask potential participants to preregister, and ask that they indicate their role preference (reader, designer, backstage, etc.).

CHOOSE ACTIVITIES Readers' theater programs work well as a series of sessions over a span of several weeks. The performance is the final session. Activities for each session are focused on preparing for the final performance and include group and individual reading practice, construction of props and costumes, and performance movement and blocking practice.

PREPARE ACTIVITY MATERIALS There are some materials you will want to prepare prior to the first practice session. Books or scripts, for example, should be prepared for use by participants before the first practice. Scripts can be printed and placed in black folders so as not to be visually distracting during the performance. Consider having a few quiet games, puzzles, or other activities for children to do when other participants might be practicing their lines.

During the Program

FIRST PROGRAM SESSION At the beginning of the first program session, distribute books or scripts along with practice and performance schedules. Assign individual parts and jobs to participants, and begin the process of reading through the script together as a group.

REMAINING SESSIONS Begin each session by distributing scripts, and begin reading through the script together. Distribute pencils and encourage participants to make notes on their scripts as needed. Ask participants to label their script with their name so that they receive the same script each time. Devote a portion of each practice to working on props, backdrops, and costumes as needed. Use the final practice as a dress rehearsal and run straight through the script without stopping.

Closing the Program

PREPARE PARTICIPANTS As you end each practice session, collect all scripts in order to make sure they are available for the next practice. Remind participants of practice sessions as well as the schedule for the final performance. Remind participants to invite friends and family to the performance. Provide information or tickets for participants to share with friends and family.

Play-Based Program
for Kindergarten through Second Grade

Before the Program

CHOOSE ACTIVITIES Activities should foster imaginative play and social skills, such as turn-taking, sharing, and cooperation. Make props available for younger children to use during dramatic play. For game-based programs, choose board games, video games and applications, or card games that are developmentally appropriate. For gross motor–based programs, choose movement activities that are feasible for participants in your target age range and that are appropriate for the space. For Lego block building programs, choose block sets that are appropriate for the age of your participants.

PLAN THE NUMBER OF PARTICIPANTS The number of participants will be determined by the type of play-based program that you choose to offer. For programs focusing on dramatic play, you will want to cap your program at a number that is appropriate for the space size and the noise level of your activity. For game-based programs, limit the number of participants to a comfortable number of players per game. For programs emphasizing gross motor skills, the amount of space you have available will determine the number of participants—larger programs can take place outdoors if you have outdoor space available. Lego building program participants should be capped at a comfortable number according to your space and the amount of Legos you have available.

PREPARE ACTIVITY MATERIALS It is important to prepare materials and supplies prior to the beginning of your play-based program. For programs with interactive stations, be sure to set up the room beforehand and encourage participants to circulate from station to station. Be sure that all games, puzzles, or block sets are in good repair and are not missing pieces.

During the Program

WELCOME AND INTRODUCTION Welcome participants and explain the play-based activities that are available. Explain the procedure for choosing an activity as well as the procedure for moving from activity to activity.

PROGRAM ACTIVITIES If participants can move from activity to activity, be sure to give a countdown and cue participants when it is time to move on to the next activity. Ask participants to return game pieces, toys, and blocks to their original location before moving to another station. Having items in their original order will help the next participants jump right into play as they begin the new activity. Place books and other materials for checkout in an area to be reviewed by program participants. Choose display materials that connect directly to the areas of play that are represented by your program activities.

Closing the Program

PREPARE PARTICIPANTS It is especially important to provide a countdown as your program approaches the end of the allotted time. This reminder helps children transition and gives them the opportunity to wrap up their own activities. Distribute information regarding upcoming play-based programs, and consider distributing surveys so participants can express interest in other play-based programs for the future.

Family/Multigenerational Program

Before the Program

CHOOSE ACTIVITIES Activities should be appropriate for all ages. Consider the safety of materials for younger participants and the interest levels of the various ages that will be represented. Choose activities that encourage interaction between and within families and that foster literacy skills.

PLAN THE NUMBER OF PARTICIPANTS Keep in mind that you will have more participants who are attending together as a family. If you offer preregistration, ask those signing up to indicate the number of family members who will attend the program. Consider limiting the number of families to best fit the space that you have available and to suit the amount of time and materials that will be required for your activities.

PREPARE ACTIVITY MATERIALS If you will be offering craft activities as part of your program, keep in mind that the process of creating is more important for children than creating a perfect product. If you will be including games or other activities in your program, make sure that all pieces are included and set up as many of the games as needed prior to the program. Prepare materials and books that you will use during whole-group activities. As with any type of program, it is better to plan more activities than you think you might need rather than risk running out of things to do. You never know how a program may change according to the interest levels of participants.

During the Program

WELCOME AND INTRODUCTION Welcome all participants at the door and explain where they should sit. Distribute any written instructions or handouts at the door as the participants enter. Explain how the program will work and the order for the program. Encourage all members of the family to participate in all parts of the program. Remind participants that this program is for everyone in the family.

PROGRAM ACTIVITIES It is important to offer a variety of activities during family programs. Plan different types of activities of varying levels of difficulty. This approach will ensure that you are offering something for everyone—activities that meet the varying abilities and interests represented by the families attending your program. Offer some activities that are intended for everyone to do together as a group, such as games, songs, and stories. Whole-group activities encourage families to interact with other families and help children interact with their peers. In addition to providing whole-group activities, it is important to offer activities that can be completed within individual families. These activities can be set up as stations around the room that families can complete after the whole-group activities are completed. Activity stations might include games, experiments, crafts, building projects, or reading aloud together.

Closing the Program

PREPARE PARTICIPANTS As with any program that includes activity stations, participants in multigenerational programs should be given a countdown of time remaining as they work at the stations. These reminders give families the opportunity to complete projects together before they move to other activities and to wrap up their work together before the close of the program. Consider asking families to share their thoughts on future programs that they would like to attend together at the library. You might obtain this feedback through informal conversations as families leave the program, or you might want to distribute comment cards or brief surveys that families can either fill out immediately or bring back to the library at another time.

Sensory/Special Needs Program

Before the Program

CHOOSE ACTIVITIES When planning activities for children with sensory issues or other special needs, it is important to choose activities that are not overwhelming or overly stimulating. Dimmed lighting and soft music are helpful for children with special needs. It is also important to plan for specific transitions between activities. Transitions can be made easier by using visual cues to announce upcoming transitions. Visual schedules with images that represent each activity can help prepare children for upcoming changes as you move together through the program.

PLAN THE NUMBER OF PARTICIPANTS It is important to keep the group size small when planning a program for children with special needs. Large groups are often overwhelming because of crowding and noise level issues. To help keep the group small, it is best to plan more than one program if interest warrants. It is also important to provide adequate space to ensure that participants have plenty of room to sit and move comfortably.

PREPARE ACTIVITY MATERIALS When planning activities, it is important to choose materials that will not overwhelm the senses of children with special needs. Limit the number of choices to just a couple of options, and choose items that are not extreme in temperature or texture. Choose items that are not overly bright but that are easy to discriminate from table surfaces. When choosing materials that participants will use, keep in mind the individual needs and abilities of the children who will be attending the program.

During the Program

WELCOME AND INTRODUCTION Welcome children and caregivers at the door. Keep lighting and music soft as children enter. Have comfortable seating ready for children, and softly explain to caregivers the format of the program. Show the children the visual schedule with images of each part of the program represented. Explain the method that will be used for moving through each part of the visual schedule.

PROGRAM ACTIVITIES As you move through each activity, remove the corresponding image from the visual schedule. Remember to do all the activities in the specific order that you have planned them and in the order in which they appear on the visual schedule. Following routines and meeting expectations are particularly important for children with special needs. When possible, provide each child with individual copies of books that you read to the entire group, and provide handouts with lyrics to songs and rhymes.

Closing the Program

PREPARE PARTICIPANTS As with each part of the program, it is important to prepare children with special needs for the close of the program. Provide plenty of extra time for children who may take longer to wrap up their activities. Close the program the same way each time. This consistency helps children anticipate the way the program will end, which helps children with special needs ease into the end of the program each time.

6

Specialized Group Programs and Outreach Services

DELIVERING SPECIALIZED PROGRAMS IS AN IMPORTANT PART of children's programming. Although many library programs are intended for individual children and families, programs for schools and other groups are just as important. In this chapter, we will take a look at strategies for linking specialized group programs to literacy and reading skill development.

In-House Programs for Special Groups

There are many ways that your library can work with groups to create specialized in-house programs that best meet the specific needs of those groups. These programs might include field trips, after-school programs at the library, school-sponsored family programs, homeschool programs, or informational programs for families. Let's take a look at the variables that you should consider in planning in-house programs for special groups.

FIELD TRIPS

When collaborating with schools and other community organizations to provide in-house programs or field trips at the library, it is important to gather information that will help you meet the individual needs of the group. Throughout this book, we have covered the important role that surveys can play during the planning stage of children's programming. Surveys are a useful tool for planning field trips as well. Surveys can be sent directly to the teacher or leader of the group asking for information on the purpose and goals of the field trip. Ask why the group is visiting the public library and what types of materials participants will be seeking. In the survey, ask the teacher or group leader if there are specific services that you might be able to provide that the school library media center or the organization might not be able to provide. Consider contacting the school librarian to ask how the public library might be able to help the specific group while promoting a collaborative relationship with the school library media center. Building a working relationship with school librarians is important to meeting the needs of students in your community.

Field trips may have general or specific objectives. Teachers may simply want students to become more familiar with the public library and learn how to find materials. For this type of visit, or as an initial visit, consider providing a tour of the library focusing on how materials are organized within the collection. For children in kindergarten through second grade, keep your explanation simple, reviewing the different areas of the collection that the children might need to access. Explain how the shelves are organized and how the children can find materials on the shelves. Discuss the differences between fiction and nonfiction, and explain how each is categorized within the library's collection. Show the students the library's online catalog, and demonstrate how they can use it to search for materials. Do this demonstration for a few students at a time, or, if your library has a large enough computer lab, provide a demonstration to all the students at once. After the demonstration, students can practice using the catalog to search for various items on their own. As students practice finding items using the online catalog, assist them in locating the items on the shelves. This hands-on practice helps young children in kindergarten through second grade make connections between the online catalog and materials that are a part of the library's collection.

A more in-depth review of search terms using the online catalog can be used with children in third through fifth grade. As you demonstrate how to use the online catalog, show students how to limit subject areas and collections in order to narrow down their searches, and follow up by encouraging students to look for the materials on the shelves. Review the Dewey Decimal Classification system and any other classification systems that your library might use and then provide a tour of each area of the collection, pointing out how the materials are organized on the shelves. Linking these activities together during the same visit to the library will help students better understand how to find materials on their own. Be sure to point out that the library's online catalog can also be accessed from school and the students' homes.

In addition to teaching students how to use the catalog to locate and access materials in the library, it is appropriate to offer story-based field trip programs for students in kindergarten through second grade. Story-based programs can offer literacy-based enrichment for students and can support content that is being covered at school. Discuss core content and classroom curriculum with the teacher prior to the field trip in order to choose books that support or expand on what the students are learning. Story-based programs may also include information about how to use the library and how to behave appropriately while visiting the library, as well as information about checkout policies and procedures. Activities such as games and arts and crafts can also be included during field trips, if time permits.

Field trips for students in third through fifth grade may also include information about library use and procedures for checking out materials. This information can be coupled with a tour of the collection and a review of how to use checkout stations, online catalogs, and public computers. A program that takes a more in-depth look at the Dewey Decimal Classification system or other classification systems used by the library may also be appropriate. When creating materials and activities for a classification system program for tweens, prepare a handout or presentation with information on how the classification system works and how this scheme translates to the organization of the materials on the library's shelves. Be sure to include information on the subject areas included in each section of the nonfiction collection on a handout for students to take with them after the program.[1] Printed handouts will help students review the information and possibly locate materials in their school library as well. Prior to planning a program that focuses on classification systems, touch base with the school librarian or media specialist to make sure you are providing information that also relates to the school library's classification system.

In addition to providing information about using your library's materials, tools, and classification systems, make sure that your field trip program inspires tweens to read. One activity that can help you foster interest in reading with tweens is a booktalk. A booktalk is a brief summary of a book that ends with an open-ended hook to help build interest and curiosity, a technique that works especially well with reluctant or struggling readers. Booktalks can include text from the book or the publisher's description on the back or flap of the book. Presenting booktalks and summaries in a dramatic voice helps "sell" books to listeners by piquing their interest. It is important not to give away too much of the story when presenting a booktalk, but include enough information to make listeners want to know what happens. The goal should be to lead students to books that they are excited about reading. Many online sites offer help with creating booktalks, including publisher websites, author websites, and resource blogs.[2] Before you plan the books that you will booktalk during a field trip, ask the teacher about the interest levels of the students and about what types of books the class needs to read for upcoming assignments.

Create booktalks that are fun and interesting, but also choose books that meet the reading levels of the students and connect to the content of the classroom curriculum.

Field trips represent one type of program that your library might develop for specialized groups. The following sections present several other types of programs that your library should consider offering through collaborative partnerships with schools and other organizations within your community.

AFTER-SCHOOL PROGRAMS AT THE LIBRARY

After-school programs that you host at the library can include daily homework help sessions, book discussion groups, or activity-based clubs. Homework help sessions might include face-to-face help from staff or volunteers, or your library might consider subscribing to an online tutoring service, such as Tutor.com (www.tutor.com/libraries) or Brainfuse (http://home.brainfuse .com/libraries). If your library offers tutoring services after school, it is important to provide a quiet space that is large enough for participants to work. In addition, tutors need to be knowledgeable in the subject areas in which they are providing assistance. Your library will want to stay current with the content and curriculum of schools in your community. It is also important to offer training for staff who will be responsible for leading the tutoring and homework help programs.

Online tutoring can be offered through the library's computer lab, or library patrons need to be able to access the service at home through the library's website or via a mobile app. By subscribing to an online tutoring service, your library will be able to provide tutoring during specified hours of service. Some online services are available twenty-four hours per day, while others may be offered only during specific hours. Subscription fees for libraries vary among services and may include various levels of service. It is important to determine the level and hours of need for your library's community prior to subscribing. Surveys can be useful for gathering this information from potential users and can be distributed at the library, at schools, and through your library's website.

In addition to homework help and tutoring services, another type of after-school program that your library might want to consider is a book discussion group. This type of program can be tailored to fit the needs and interests of the participants. Programs can be planned in collaboration with schools in your library's community or with other after-school service organizations. Books that are chosen for after-school book clubs can include books that are included on school reading lists, such as Battle of the Books or other supplemental reading lists.[3] Book discussion groups may be offered for specific grades and may be designed for children to attend on their own or with their parents and caregivers. Book discussion groups should engage children in discussion of the plot and themes of the book. Hands-on activities that connect to the book's themes and vocabulary should be integrated to help make the text more concrete for participants and support comprehension skills. Book discussion programs also offer opportunities for social and language development.

In addition to after-school homework help and book discussion groups, activity-based clubs are another option that can be tailored to the specific needs of target groups. Your library might consider offering crafting clubs, technology-based clubs, or interest-based clubs. A club-based program belongs to the participants. It is important to encourage participants to take leadership of the activities that are included. In this way, library staff members serve as program facilitators rather than as leaders of the program. The club-based program draws on the interests of participants, with activities being adapted by the members to best fit their needs. Club program sessions may take place weekly, biweekly, or monthly and work well as afternoon or evening program options.

SCHOOL-SPONSORED FAMILY LITERACY EVENTS

In addition to school field trips and after-school programs, public libraries often host family literacy events designed for specific schools. Family literacy events can be uniquely designed to meet the needs of a specific school, classroom, or group. When planning a program with the intention of promoting family literacy, it is important to gather information through working directly with the participating school. Ask teachers and other school service providers to share what they know about the literacy needs and abilities of the families and children at their school. Discuss with school representatives whether they would like you to offer a family literacy event for all families from the school or for specific families by invitation. Also discuss the format that the representatives would like the program to follow.

There are many different formats or types of programs that you may choose to use. A story-based program is one format that works well for school-sponsored family literacy events. Story-based programs can also include interactive components, such as arts and crafts, science-based activities, or games that encourage teamwork. All activities included in family literacy programs are intended to promote literacy in the home. The importance of reading is emphasized, and best practices should be intentionally modeled, just as with any program. As you plan the family literacy program, be sure to incorporate activities that foster each of the modes of multiliteracy. Introduce technology that cultivates visual, textual, and digital media literacy. Provide opportunities for social interaction within and between families who attend the program, and incorporate hands-on activities that include multisensory experiences. In this way, your family literacy program will be intentionally linked to best practices that can be used at home. In addition to family literacy events for schools, your library can offer programs for homeschool groups.

HOMESCHOOL PROGRAMS

The number of homeschool cooperative groups has increased dramatically among homeschooling populations over recent years. These groups often meet at various locations for educational and social enrichment. Some homeschool groups have lessons that are taught by parents and caregivers for children of specific ages and grade levels. Your library might offer to lead programs that would support specific topics that are a part of the homeschool curriculum used by the group. You may ask special presenters from the community to collaborate with you, depending on the topic of a program, or library staff may lead the program. Library programs that incorporate hands-on experiential activities are particularly useful to homeschool groups. It is important to host programs with activities in a space that is large enough for the entire group to meet together.

In addition to offering stand-alone programs for homeschool groups, your library might provide ongoing programs that you also offer for the public but that are adapted to fit the needs of homeschool groups. Most of the programs we covered in chapter 4 can be adapted to meet the specific needs of homeschool groups, including book clubs, story-based programs, STEAM programs, Battle of the Books, and readers' theater. When your library maintains an open dialogue with homeschool group leaders, it is easier to stay in tune with the needs of the group. If you have not reached out to members of homeschool groups in your community, try inviting them to meet in order to discuss the programs that the library could sponsor to help support the educational and literacy-based goals of their groups.

PARENT AND CAREGIVER INFORMATIONAL PROGRAMS

In addition to offering family literacy events and programs for homeschool groups, your library might want to consider providing informational programs for parents and caregivers to attend without children. Informational programs for adults may include such topics as literacy and reading practices or behavior and child development, or you may want to invite a speaker to address a specific parenting concern. When hosting informational programs for adults, be sure to promote materials from the library's collection that support the program's topic, such as informational resource books or materials that are intended for use with children.

Informational programs for adults can include multiple sessions or be offered as single, stand-alone programs. Gathering information from potential participants prior to planning will help you decide which format is the most appropriate for your audience. If you are cosponsoring the program with an organization or a school, you can ask for assistance in distributing interest surveys to potential participants along with making them available online. Another option might be to hold an introductory session for parents and caregivers and ask participants to complete a needs survey at the close of the session. This survey can be used to help you plan future program topics and select speakers who align with the needs of the participants.

Informational programs for adults can be offered at the library, at schools, or at other locations throughout the community. If you collaborate with your community's health department, staff members may have already established specific family programming sites in the community. This approach will help you reach populations that you may not reach by hosting the program at the library. Health department staff can also help you identify the best time and location for your program as well as topics that might be most useful for parents and caregivers who might attend. If you work with schools to organize an informational program, you will have a ready-made audience comprising the school's parents and caregivers. Think about other service providers from your community that can help you reach parents and caregivers whom you might not see regularly at the library—for example, grandparents raising their grandchildren, or teen parents. Keep in mind that it may be difficult for some adults to attend programs without bringing their children. If your library has the staff and space to offer simultaneous programs, you can offer a program for children in a separate room while the program for adults is presented. If you are working with another organization and hosting the program at a different location, ask if space is available for simultaneous programs. Some organizations may also be able to arrange child care if your library does not have staff available to lead two programs at once. The goals of informational programs for adults should be to reach underserved populations and to serve the needs of parents and caregivers in your community. Offering solutions such as simultaneous programs or child care may go a long way toward helping you reach these goals and increase attendance.

Group Outreach Services

In addition to cosponsoring informational programs for adults with organizations in your community, your library will want to consider providing specialized outreach services to groups that serve children throughout the community. Service organizations might include groups that provide programs for after-school care or school clubs, community recreational centers, or public housing communities. Connecting with these service organizations offers your library the opportunity to work with already established groups of children that you may not be currently serving. When planning specialized outreach programs, it is important to connect to the needs and interests of the specific audience. Any activities that you include should be easy to replicate by group leaders after your program. Outreach program topics and structures might look similar to those for programs that your library would offer in-house. Before planning an outreach program, you should visit the location to evaluate the environment and the logistics for the activities and materials you will include in the program.

If your library can check out materials to patrons during outreach programs, make sure to provide enough time for checkout during the program. Checkout procedures should also match the needs of the specific group. Patrons who check out materials during an outreach program should be able to return items during an upcoming outreach program. If your library has the budget to provide a separate collection of paperback books for outreach programs, this option can minimize the impact on the in-house collection. These small collections are easier to transport and can be replaced at a lower cost than most books in the regular collection.

Library outreach programs that are planned for students in after-school care at elementary schools may be delivered through a variety of formats, depending on the number and grade range of the program's participants. Book discussion groups can work for a variety of grade levels if your library is able to supply enough copies of the book for each reader. Shorter books can be read during the session and discussed, or books might even be read aloud and discussed. Extension activities, including crafts or experiential activities, can tie real-world knowledge to the content presented in the books read by the group. If your library provides a book-based program in partnership with an after-school group sponsored by a school, you may want to consider working together to supply materials for hands-on projects. After-school groups may already have budgets in place for materials, or you may consider applying for a partnership grant that would help pay for materials.

In addition to after-school care, schools may sponsor clubs that take place during the school day or during the summer, such as lunchtime book discussion groups.[4] These programs are often facilitated by teachers and school librarians, and students are invited to participate during their lunchtime. Teachers who know the students well choose the participants, which makes it possible for students to be chosen based on their needs and abilities. Public library staff can support lunchtime discussion groups by supplying copies of the chosen book, and librarians can attend or lead specific sessions. Public library staff can also contribute to supportive activities that reinforce the concepts addressed in the book. Field trips to the public library may be included at some point during the program to introduce the library's services and collections to students who have not previously visited.

In addition to school-sponsored programs, your library may consider offering programs at community recreational centers. These centers often serve latchkey children or those who live in poverty and may be at risk for academic failure. These children may not be likely to visit the library with their families. Providing outreach programs at these centers can help your library reach at-risk and underserved children. Programs that involve book discussion or story-based activities can work well at recreational centers because they often serve a wide age range. Hands-on activities can support literacy-based programs at recreational centers. Discuss activity plans prior to the program with the leaders of the program. Ask about the materials that they may be able to supply. If the library needs to provide materials for activities, be sure to choose materials that are easy and small enough to transport. Be flexible with your plans. Be ready to adapt activities as needed to accommodate any changes that may occur with the participants or location. It is more important that participants engage in activities that foster literacy skills than it is that you follow every detail of your lesson plan.

Public housing communities offer another opportunity for outreach programming. Most public housing areas have recreational centers on-site. These centers sometimes offer programs for children and families living in the community, including family literacy programs, child-care services, and special events. Most often, a staff is responsible for scheduling events and coordinating programs for families that live in the public housing community. Reach out to staff members in order to determine the community's literacy needs and ask if your library can offer a program using on-site facilities. This approach offers you another opportunity to reach families and children who may not be able to visit the library. As with any other specialized program, you will want to tailor your activities to meet the needs and abilities that are present in the community that you are serving.

We have covered several types of specialized groups and outreach programs that you will want to consider in order to reach underserved groups of children in kindergarten through fifth grade. In addition to these specialized groups, your library should offer large events that are intended for the entire community. In the next chapter, we will take a look at the steps involved in planning for large events and summer reading programs.

NOTES

1. Online Computer Library Center, "Resources for Teachers and Students of the DDC," https://www.oclc.org/dewey/resources/public.en.html.

2. Scholastic, "Booktalks," www.scholastic.com/teacher/ab/booktalks.htm.

3. Battle of the Books, "What Is BOB?" http://battleofthebooks.com/what-is-bob/.

4. Jenifer Rank, "Lunch Bunch Book Clubs: A Model Fostering the Love of Reading," *Illinois Reading Council Journal* 41, no. 2 (2013): 22–27.

7

Large Event and Summer Reading Program Planning

ALTHOUGH MOST PROGRAMS OFFERED BY THE PUBLIC LIBRARY are intended for specific groups of patrons, large events that are appropriate for all ages represent another type of program that is sponsored by the children's department. Large events may be cosponsored by the library and other community organizations, or they may be sponsored and hosted solely by the library. Large events often involve working with guest presenters or special topics. Special events that draw large crowds may be offered more than once in order to serve the most patrons. Programs that are offered more than once should be scheduled during different times of the day or evening to meet the scheduling needs of potential participants.

Guest Presenters

When planning programs that involve guest presenters, you will have to deal with special circumstances, depending on the type of presenter and the type of program you would like to offer. Guest presenters might include individuals from your state or local community, or they may be national or international performers. See the accompanying text box for a list of sources of potential presenters. Before you contact individuals about the possibility of presenting a program through the library, you should put together a list of possible dates and times that fit within the library's overall schedule. Once you have such a list, you will want to look at your program budget. It is helpful to have an approximate fee range in mind prior to contacting potential presenters. Some presenters publish their fee schedule on their website, while others ask that you contact them with your needs before providing a fee estimate. Many state library systems publish a list of guest presenters and performers that includes a brief review of the quality of services along with the fees paid. This type of list can be quite helpful as you seek potential presenters because colleagues from other libraries are writing the reviews based on similar programming needs.

It is also important to ask guest presenters and performers to sign an agreement that stipulates the conditions and expectations for the event. This form should include such information as the date and location of the program, any materials and equipment that the library will need to supply, the materials and equipment that the presenter will need to supply, and the maximum number of participants. Any contingency plans should also be outlined in the agreement, such as cancellation procedures and rescheduling policies in the event of cancellation. The fee and payment expectations should be included on the form along with any specific requests, such as for travel, food, and lodging. You will find a Large Event Presentation Agreement in the appendix that can be reproduced for use with guest presenters or used as a reference for creating your library's own form.

Performers that your library might host as part of a large event may include musicians, magicians, theater groups, comedians, or variety acts. It is important to choose the location, date, and time that best align with the type of performance and the needs of the performers. Before you send the presentation agreement to your presenter(s), you will want to have a verbal agreement on the venue, fees, and date that the program will be offered. This informal arrangement will help ensure that the most significant details are agreed upon by both sides before a formal agreement is signed.

Author Visits

Another type of large event program that involves working with a special guest is an author visit. Author visits can be sponsored and hosted solely by the library or in collaboration with schools or other community organizations. Community-wide or school-based programs can be planned to help promote a large event with the author at the close of the program. In chapter 4 we looked at several examples of community-wide book initiatives, including those that are linked to author visits. When planning a community-wide book initiative that includes a visit by an author, you will want to choose one or two books written by the author as the focus of your program. It is important to plan activities that correlate with the themes and content of the featured books. It is especially helpful if these books are relevant to your potential audience and to the community in which your library is located. Choosing a book that includes relevant themes, characters, or story lines that represent your com-

Large Event Presenter Sources

Acting Troupes

- Local, state, and national acting troupes provide theater performances and acting workshops.

Animals

- Local groups provide programs with trained service animals, such as reading to dogs or cats.
- Local, state, and national animal groups, zoos, and aquariums travel with various animals to provide live animal shows.

Artists

- Local, regional, and national crafters, painters, pottery artists, textile artists, and drawing artists and illustrators provide demonstrations and hands-on workshops.

Authors

- Local and national authors travel to speak, lead hands-on writing workshops, and visit schools.

Characters in Costumes

- Local and regional companies supply costumes and people who will travel to programs dressed as specific characters.

Comedians

- Local and national comedians travel to present live comedy shows for children and families.

Computer Programmers

- Local computer programmers teach coding and game design.

Cultural Topics and Languages

- Local groups provide performances and hands-on workshops featuring various cultural practices and traditions as well as storytimes based on specific languages.

Dancers

- Local dance studios provide performances and workshops that teach dance techniques.

Educational Topics

- Local colleges and universities provide hands-on workshops on science.
- Local nature reserves and state parks present programs on local animals and habitats.
- Local banks present financial literacy workshops.

Extension Agents

- Community extension agents present educational workshops on a variety of topics, including agriculture, the environment, nutrition and cooking, and livestock.

Gaming

- Video game trucks and gaming companies travel to libraries and provide equipment and workshops based on specific games.
- Large game companies set up and service giant board games, climbing equipment, and inflatables.

Health and Fitness

- Local health and fitness companies offer exercise and athletic demonstrations and training for a wide variety of physical activities, including jazzercise, Zumba, parkour, yoga, running, swimming, bicycling, and hiking.

History Centers

- Local history centers offer workshops and presentations about the history of your community. Cultural information, artifacts, and hands-on activities are often included. History centers that have community rooms may offer space for large collaborative programs.

Local Community Workers and Specialists

- Local police officers, firefighters, and other emergency workers present programs on safety and will often bring trucks and cars for families to explore.

Continued on page 90

- Local bakeries and chefs provide baking, cake decorating, and cooking classes that would be appropriate for families.
- Local gardening clubs present workshops on gardening and composting for families.
- Local interest groups and clubs will often partner with libraries to present programs on specific interests, such as robotics, chess, card games, or collecting.

Magicians

- Local and national magicians present large magic shows for children and families as well as hands-on workshops for children.

Martial Arts

- Martial arts studios in your community may be willing to present a martial arts program at your library or at their studios.

Museums

- Local museums offer collaborative programs in their own spaces and may be able to bring specific materials to the library for a program for children and families.

Musicians

- Musicians in your community may be willing to perform at a large program for families. Many are also able to provide hands-on workshops for children.
- National musical performers will travel and perform at your large event for a fee, which usually includes mileage or travel expenses, accommodations, and meals.

Parks and Recreation

- Your community's parks and recreation department can make a great partner for large events. Outdoor space may be available to the library at no cost, and the department may have staff who would

be able to present large outdoor programs for free, such as tennis, golf, volleyball, hiking, disc golf, swimming, geocaching, or other outdoor recreational programs.

Photographers and Videographers

- Local photographers may present workshops on various types of photography. Photographers may also be hired to take family pictures at special large events.
- Videographers in your community may be willing to present workshops on techniques such as stop-motion or on making videos or video book trailers.

Puppetry

- Puppeteers may be local or a traveling troupe and may present a large performance for families and children. Some may also offer hands-on puppet-building workshops.

Sports Teams and Coaches

- Local sports teams and coaches may be willing to present a sports clinic. This type of program works well during summer reading if outdoor space is needed. Local high school teams or other teen leagues may be willing to offer a workshop for children at the library, a local gym, or other venue.

Storytellers

- Most communities have storytellers. Some storytellers offer traditional or folktale performances, while others may offer workshops for children who are interested in learning how to write and perform stories.

munity can help you reach out to community organizations to create program partnerships. These partnerships can lead to cosponsored activities that are offered to the community as part of your library's community-wide book initiative and author visit.

Mock Award Events

Another large event that you can invite the community to participate in is a mock book awards program. This program can be tied to the Newbery and Caldecott book awards, and activities can span several months.[1] Children in the community can choose books to read from a suggested list and then collectively choose which books they feel will win the book awards at the ceremony sponsored each January by the American Library Association.[2] Your library can serve as the central voting location after children have read the books. The mock awards events can be planned in collaboration with community schools, and your library can host the live webcast of the awards.[3] Your library can work with school librarians in order to choose the number of students who will attend the awards webcast. This number will depend partially on the size of the space you have available, but the school librarians can also help by forming awards clubs or committees in their schools. The students who participate in the school-based clubs may then attend the awards webcast program at your library. If the space at your library is not adequate for a large awards event, consider collaborating with a school or other community organization that has enough space to host the large event.

Summer Reading Programs

Although your library will likely host many large events throughout the year, summer reading usually includes many large events over a short period. Most summer reading programs last anywhere from four to eight weeks and include regular storytime sessions in addition to several large programs for all ages. The overall goal of library summer reading programs is to lessen the impact of summer slide, or the loss of reading and other learning skills that might occur over the summer months.[4] In addition to programs, summer reading includes a reading component, usually in the form of a reading log that tracks the number of books a participant reads over the summer. Small prizes are usually awarded to participants for completing reading logs, and many libraries award grand prizes from a drawing of all summer reading participants' names. Program attendance may also be required as part of the summer reading log completion and might include storytime, in-house, outreach, and large event attendance. As you plan programs that are part of your library's summer reading, choose activities that support literacy development and encourage reading. Large events that are part of your summer reading schedule can include any type of program that is offered at any other time of the year. Your large programs may simply be on a larger scale during the summer because your library will likely have a larger summer reading program audience. This possibility makes summer a good time to feature more well-known presenters or those who will likely draw a large crowd.

As with any program that incorporates a guest presenter, you will want to ask presenters to complete a program agreement. It is especially important during the library's busy summer program schedule to be sure that you have program plans in place, materials ready, and any venues that are needed outside the library arranged in plenty of time. Remember to check your state library's website for guest presenter lists and meet with other libraries to share information about performers and presenters. Library systems that are located within the same region may want to work together to book traveling performers on the same day or week. This collaboration may help lower costs or ensure that your library is able to book presenters who are willing to travel farther because they will be performing at more than one library.

Another type of guest presenter that you might want to consider working with during summer reading programs is the community presenter. These presenters might include local artists, community service providers, recreational service providers, local celebrities, or content area experts. When working with local presenters, it is important to look for ways that a mutually beneficial partnership can be formed beyond the single program. Such partnerships promote the presenters' services to your patrons while increasing interest in the library's program because the presenters are local.

In addition to providing regular storytime programs and working with guest presenters during the summer, you will want to offer large events that are planned solely by the library. These events can be held at the library or at satellite locations throughout the community. A large summer reading kick-off event can be presented for patrons who register to participate in the summer reading log program. A large summer reading promotional program like this can help boost the number of patrons who register to complete a reading log during the summer. Large kick-off programs can include numerous activities that can be done outdoors. If your library has a large outdoor space, rental companies offer games and activities that can be used during your event, and many companies will also send staff to help set up and supervise the larger activities. This benefit is particularly helpful if you have several large activities and a large crowd.

In addition to hosting a large kick-off event for summer reading, your library may cohost large summer reading events throughout the community. Large events that take place at various locations open up new opportunities to build partnerships with other community organizations. Such partnerships can provide larger physical spaces, help your library connect with underserved populations, and promote the services of both organizations. Community organizations that work well as partners for large summer reading events might include your county's parks and recreation department, elementary schools, or colleges in your community. It's important to ask about the ways that your library can help promote the services that your community partners provide. This promotion helps ensure a continuing partnership that best serves the community and is mutually beneficial.

Program Preparation

Specific preparations need to be made for large events. Some preparations will need to be made whether your large event takes place at the library or at another location as an outreach program. Other preparations will depend on the type and size of the program. With any type of large program, it is a good rule of thumb to develop a planning outline or checklist to help guide your planning efforts. Large events often include several small details, and a planning outline can help ensure that each one is done according to a specific time line. You might choose to develop your own checklist according to each of the steps that are involved in preparing for the program. One of the program planning outlines in chapter 5 is specifically formulated to be used for author visits and guest presenter programs. A Large Event Program Planning Checklist template can be found in the appendix, along with suggested planning surveys, to help guide each step of the large event planning process.

It is important to assign specific tasks to staff members and volunteers who may be helping prepare for the large event. Using a planning checklist can help you keep track of each task and when it is complete. A program checklist can include lists of items to be purchased, working time lines and deadlines for completion of tasks, and contact information for any partners or special guests who may be part of your library's large event. Any changes that occur during the planning phase can be recorded on the checklist along with any necessary deadline adjustments.

For large programs that require materials to be prepared ahead of time, it is helpful to have an estimated number of participants prior to the program. Requiring preregistration is the best way to plan for an approximate number of participants, allowing you to prepare materials to meet the level of interest. Even with preregistration, it is good practice to prepare a few extra sets of materials in order to be best prepared for the unexpected, including siblings who might attend the program or children who use more materials than expected. For programs that take place at the library, it is helpful to place project supplies on the tables along with any instructions that might be needed. Table tents with brief instructions work well without taking up too much space. Simply type brief step-by-step instructions and print them centered in the middle of the paper. Fold the top and bottom of the paper in toward the center, dividing the paper into thirds with the instructions appearing in the middle section. The resulting triangular table tent can then stand on the table. In order to encourage creative expression, do not provide any examples of the finished project. When you provide examples, children will often strive to emulate what you have done rather than work to create their own original projects. Hands-on projects that are used to reinforce the theme should focus on the process of the experience and the opportunity for learning more about the subject matter of the program. Although it is helpful to prepare supplies prior to the program, examples not only are unnecessary but also can prevent participants from having the best experience possible.

Space and Venue Considerations

In addition to scheduling and preparing materials, it is important to choose the best space or venue for your library's large event. If needed, events that take place at the library can be offered multiple times, and participants can choose one session to attend. This approach allows you to serve more participants at popular programs and is especially helpful if your library does not have a space large enough to accommodate everyone who might be interested in attending. You will also want to consider the physical requirements of the activities that you will include in your program. For example, you will need to choose a space with a sink or faucet (or a space near water) for programs that require water for activities or for cleaning them up. If a program includes messy activities, you may choose to complete them in a room without carpet or even outdoors if your library has outdoor space available. Programs that include video or audio components require a space with appropriate lighting, seating, and acoustics. Appropriate audiovisual equipment needs to be available and set up prior to the program.

Furniture arrangement is another important consideration for large events. Some activities will require only chairs for participants, while other program activities will also require tables. For large events it is especially important that the furniture fits comfortably in the space. It is also important that furniture is the right size for potential participants and that enough seating is available for the number of participants who are expected to attend. Seating should be arranged so that participants can see and hear well, especially if the audience is very large.

For programs with potential audiences larger than your library's largest space, other venues can be considered, such as schools or colleges in the community, community theaters, convention centers, or outdoor areas such as parks or amphitheaters. Large events that are offered at one of these locations can be cosponsored with other community organizations. Organizations that have large spaces available for programs may be willing to donate a space for your library's large event in exchange for the free advertising and attention that your event will provide for their venue. As you consider working with large venues in your community, think about your parking needs, the needs of any presenters who will be associated with the event, and the logistics of effectively promoting the location of the event.

Assigning Roles Using a Time Line

If your library has staff members who can contribute to planning your large events, it is important to assign them specific jobs. Meet with the staff periodically and provide deadlines for completing each specific assignment. This approach ensures that the smaller details are completed along the way, keeping the project well organized.

The large event planning time line in the accompanying text box offers a suggested schedule of actions to guide your project. Details are included to help you time each step of planning a large event. These details can be changed as needed to fit your specific program.

Your time line planning form should be distributed to each staff member responsible for completing any part of the large event program plan and should include details on pre-program preparation, details to be taken care of during the program, program wrap-up details, and plans for debriefing after the program to discuss the things that worked or need to be adjusted prior to your next large event program (see the Staff Program Planning Process Survey template in the appendix). Using a time line to guide each step of planning a large event and evaluating what worked and what needs to be changed in the future will help you plan the best large event possible and help guide your library's future large events.

We have covered specific details for planning various types of programs, including programs that take place in the library, programs that are built through collaborative partnerships, and large event programs that require

Large Event Planning Time Line

Six Months Prior

- Research large events that may be of interest to your community.
- Ask patrons to complete interest surveys to help the library consider future large event programming (see the Patron Large Event Interest Survey template in the appendix).
- Determine the amount in your library's budget that can be allocated to the large event and promotional efforts.
- Consider appropriate community partners and venues.

Three Months Prior

- Contact and book presenters and venues.
- Send a presentation agreement to the presenter with a deadline for returning the form.
- Pay any required down payment or reservation fees.
- Schedule a meeting with all staff and community partners that will be involved in the large event. Begin discussing each of the details that will need to be taken care of as the event approaches. Establish a time line with deadlines.

Two Months Prior

- Stay in touch with the presenter about any additional needs for the program.
- Stay in touch with the venue to stay on the radar and to make sure all event needs will be met.
- Add the large event to the library calendar, school calendars, and community calendars.

One Month Prior

- Send out press releases to local media (television, radio, newspapers), community bulletin boards, local interest groups, and schools) and announce the event on social media.
- Release any advertisements or commercials about the upcoming event.
- Meet with staff members to update specific details. Assign responsibilities for the day of the event.
- Purchase any needed supplies and prepare any required materials.

One Week Prior

- Contact the presenter and venue to touch base and provide any updates you have on interest or registration numbers.
- Send out reminders through social media and personal invitations to community groups and the library board.
- Review the event checklist and make needed adjustments.
- Make sure final payment is ready for the presenter.
- Prepare any promotional flyers that you would like to distribute during the program for upcoming special events.

One Day Prior

- Meet with staff members to review final plans.
- Make sure all supplies are packed and ready to go.
- Double-check the presenter's travel and arrival plans.

Day of Large Event

- Review staff assignments and distribute any supplies that will be needed.
- Post signs, posters, or directions for parking at the venue.
- Greet and transport the presenter to the venue.
- Make sure everything that the presenter needs is at the venue and ready to be easily accessed as needed.

detailed planning. In the next chapter, we will take a look at planning programs for children with special needs. In order to provide the most appropriate program activities possible, you will want to intentionally consider specific details as you plan programs for children with special needs.

NOTES

1. Association for Library Service to Children, "Book and Media Awards," www.ala.org/alsc/awardsgrants/bookmedia.

2. American Library Association, "ALA Youth Media Awards," www.ala.org/news/mediapresscenter/presskits/youthmediaawards/alayouthmediaawards.

3. American Library Association, "Youth Media Awards Live Webcast," http://ala.unikron.com/.

4. Collaborative Summer Library Program, *Summer Reading White Paper,* www.cslpreads.org/.

Programming for Children with Special Needs

ALTHOUGH LIBRARY PROGRAMS FOR CHILDREN SHOULD BE open and inviting to all children, regardless of ability, many public libraries offer specialized programs designed for children with special needs and their families. These programs are offered for families that may be apprehensive about attending a program at the library because of their child's needs or behaviors. It is important to let these families know that they are welcome at the library and in all library programs. In order to pull apprehensive families into the library, programs for children with special needs, often referred to as *sensory-based programs,* are planned similarly to typical children's programs but with a few adaptations to best meet the needs of the participants. These adjustments might be made to meet the sensory, transitional, or physical needs of the children who attend the program.

Sensory Adaptations

Many environmental factors must be considered when planning a program for children with special needs. These environmental factors can have a big impact on whether a child is able to participate comfortably in a program, and these same factors can prevent a family from attending your program if conditions are not adjusted to meet the needs of your participants. For a family that is unsure about attending a program at the library because of the difficulties it might pose, you might have only one chance to prove that a library program can work for their child.

One thing that you can do to help make a positive connection with a family is to collect information about the environmental and sensory needs of their child prior to the program. The easiest way to collect such information is to send out a link to a Special Needs Program Survey (see the appendix for a template) or to distribute a paper copy of the survey. The information from the survey will help you choose activities and arrange your space to best fit the needs of your program participants.

Children who have sensory processing issues have difficulty receiving and interpreting the information that is sent to their brains from their senses.[1] Because of this difficulty in processing, children may respond to sensory input in an unusual way, impacting their behavior, ability to listen, or social interactions with others. Environmental factors can be adjusted in the library's program area in order to make sensory adaptations for children with sensory processing issues. Lighting can be dimmed for children who are overstimulated by bright lights. Music can be played softly, and any instruments that are used should be minimal. The temperature of the room should be comfortable, and any humming lights or fans should be turned off during the program. It is also a good idea to keep your group size as small as possible. Limiting the number of participants helps keep crowd noise to a minimum and provides room for participants to spread apart as needed. It is helpful to provide space at the back of the room for children who need to move freely in order to process sensory information.

Transitional Adaptations

Another program component that you will want to consider for children with special needs is the flow from one part of the program to the next. This continuity includes alternating between various types of activities and planning for the transitions that will take place between each of the activities. For some children with special needs, times of transition or change can be especially difficult. If a child with special needs has never attended a program at the library, the first visit may be particularly difficult. To help introduce a child with special needs to the library, the program space, and the staff prior to the first program, your library can post an introductory video or storybook about the library on the library's website and social media. The Libraries and Autism website offers a customizable template for libraries to create their own introductory social storybook.[2] This template can be printed and distributed, sent to participants via e-mail, or posted on your library's website. Parents and caregivers can read the story with their children to help them become familiar with the people and materials they will see at the library. This activity can help minimize the anxiety that a child with special needs might feel about visiting an unfamiliar place. It can also help parents and caregivers who may feel a bit nervous about bringing their child with special needs to a program at the library. Reaching out to families in this way can help them feel welcome at the library.

After children and families have walked through the doors of your library program, it is important that you continue to announce activity transitions to help children prepare for each new activity. One method of announcing transitions is to post a visual schedule, or a time line of pictures, to introduce each activity during the program.[3] Picture cards can be displayed on a felt or magnet board or placed in a hanging pocket chart. As each activity is completed, the associated picture is removed from the visual schedule until all activities have been completed. Using a visual schedule can help prepare children with special needs for new activities, making transitions less difficult throughout the program.

Physical Adaptations

Meeting the physical needs of your participants is another important aspect of program planning. This is especially true as you plan programs for children with special needs because physical obstacles can prevent children with special needs from attending. In order to minimize physical obstacles, it is important to collect information about the physical needs and abilities of potential participants prior to the program. This information should be collected through the Special Needs Program Survey that you distribute before the program. Physical adaptations might include seating or furniture arrangement or other adaptations to help children move or maintain the ability to sit still. Manipulatives that children can quietly fidget with during storytime can help some children focus on listening during group activities. Manipulative toys that would be appropriate for use during storytime include beanbags, stress balls, stretchy toys, and pipe cleaners.[4]

Special seating can also help children who struggle physically with sitting on the floor or in a chair because of sensory-seeking behaviors, self-regulation issues, or difficulties understanding where their body is in space. Proprioceptive dysfunction, or a child's inability to perceive how her body moves, often manifests itself through the child's inability to sit for periods of time, an inability to control her own posture, or the need for sensory input while she is sitting.[5] Special seats are available to help children who struggle with sitting still on the floor because of sensory or hyperactivity issues. These seats may provide back support, room for wiggling, or texture for sensory input.[6]

Another simple tool that can help children with proprioceptive dysfunction and sensory needs is a weighted lap pad, which looks like an extra heavy beanbag. The weighted pad is placed across a child's lap to provide deep pressure across his legs. The child can also physically manipulate the lap pad with his hands while he sits.[7] The deep pressure that the lap pad provides helps the child understand where his body is and provides the sensory input needed to help him sit. Weighted lap pads can be purchased through school or library supply companies, or they can be made by hand.

Several adaptations can be made and special supplies purchased to help children with special needs feel more comfortable attending programs at the library. It is also important that you learn as much as you can about the specific disabilities of children who attend your programs in order to prepare supplies that will be the most helpful to them.

Understanding Specific Disabilities and Disorders

It is important to have a basic understanding of specific disabilities and disorders in order to intentionally plan program activities that will meet the potential needs of the children who will attend your program. Various resources and trainings are available through state library systems, educational training providers, and online webinars. This section of the chapter provides some basic information and common characteristics of a few specific disabilities and disorders that you might encounter in programs for children with special needs. This basic knowledge is meant to help you plan your program activities, but it should not take the place of connecting directly with your participants in order to understand their personal and specific needs. It is most important that you remember that a child with special needs is first and foremost a child. The disability or special need should always come second, no matter how severe it might appear. As you plan each component of your program, use this basic information about common disabilities, but always consider the children who attend first.

AUTISM SPECTRUM DISORDER

Children with Autism Spectrum Disorder (ASD) fall somewhere on a continuum of abilities, skills, and impairments. Children with ASD are often diagnosed as toddlers when certain social behaviors are observed consistently. Various traits and behaviors become common over time, including difficulty with social interactions, repeated odd behaviors, difficulty with transitions and changes, and difficulty understanding the emotions of others.[8] Children with ASD do not all exhibit the same symptoms or the same level of severity. This is why the disorder is said to be on a spectrum. Some children on the autism spectrum may not be able to speak at all but may make vocalizations and sounds, while other children on the spectrum will be very high functioning and talk in great detail about subjects that they enjoy but without regard to social interactions. It is important to plan activities for nonverbal children as well as activities for children who have difficulty with social interactions. Although not every activity will fit the needs of every participant because of the wide range of needs and abilities of children on the autism spectrum, it is important that you are intentionally prepared to meet the variety of needs that might be represented.

Many children on the autism spectrum experience sensory processing difficulties. It is important to adapt the environment as needed to meet the sensory needs of participants. Adaptations might include adjusting the lighting, choosing quiet music or activities, or planning for a smaller group than your typical programs serve. You may also choose to incorporate activities and books that reinforce the awareness of emotions and the ability to sympathize with others, especially with children who struggle with reading their peers' emotions. Transitions and change are also often difficult for children with ASD. Activities that can be incorporated as transitions between different parts of the program are helpful for children on the autism spectrum. The visual schedule described earlier in this chapter is a great transitional tool to use with children with ASD. It is also helpful to maintain the same order of activities each week because children with ASD often do better with structure and knowing what to expect each time they attend a program. After whole-group activities, offer individual sensory-based activities at various stations around the room. Provide activities that incorporate hands-on experimentation with sensory materials, such as painting, manipulating playdough, playing with shaving cream, or playing with rice or sand on a sensory table. These types of activities expose children to sensory skill development but at their own pace. Activities that expose children to language should be planned as well, including the use of puppets or games that expose children to turn-taking and other social skills. In a well-planned, intentional program, you can provide low-stress experiences in many ways to help children practice skills that may be more difficult for them to complete because of their disability. Plan activities with the children in mind first and then, depending on the types of needs that are represented, add the adaptations to help them participate successfully.

ATTENTION DEFICIT HYPERACTIVITY DISORDER

For children with attention and hyperactivity disorders, sitting still during listening times can be difficult. Programs that incorporate movement throughout work well for children who struggle with hyperactivity. Programs that include many short activities work well for children who are not able to focus their attention on any one activity for more than a few minutes at a time. It is important to remember that just because a child is moving does not mean that she is not also listening. Children who need to move around in order to attend to whole-group activities are often able to listen better when they are able to move throughout the room as needed. Accommodating this need may mean keeping the number of participants small or providing space at the back of the room for children to move around during whole-group activities. Providing small, handheld toys for tactile manipulation may help, but there are also children who need to be able to move their whole bodies around the room in order to pay attention during group time. To the unfamiliar eye, it may appear that children who are moving about as you are reading are not listening; however, when you understand the needs of children with hyperactivity and attention disorders, you understand that it is precisely the opposite. It is important to explain this concept to all participants at the beginning of your program so that your entire group understands that just because a child is moving around does not mean that she is not listening.

In order to best meet the needs of the majority of your participants, you may find it helpful to offer two different types of programs for children with special needs. For children who have sensory processing issues, a program in which children are moving about may create too much sensory stimulation. For children who need to move, a program that is low-key with soft music and lighting may not provide the sensory input that they need in order to pay attention. If you find that you have children within a wide range of needs, consider offering a quiet program for children with sensory needs and a high-energy version of the program for children with activity-based needs. Distributing a Special Needs Program Survey can help you collect this information prior to the program, but you may also observe these needs during a single program. If so, talk to parents and caregivers after the program. This discussion helps calm any concerns that might have come up for parents and caregivers during the program and helps families feel that they remain welcome. Knowing that the library wants to best meet their child's needs can go a long way toward their continued attendance.

OTHER IMPAIRMENTS

Although the majority of children who attend your programs for children with special needs might fall within one of the two types of special needs just discussed, you may also have children with various other needs. It is important to connect with families on a level that helps you best understand the needs of the individual child. The Special Needs Program Survey can help you do this, but it is no substitute for getting to know the child and family. Talking with the family is the best way to discover what you can do during a program to meet the specific needs of their child.

Children may have physical needs that require adaptations in your program space or access to the room. Your library should already be aware of laws and regulations concerning access to the building, but there may be additional adaptations that you can provide to help meet the physical needs of the children.[9] Any adaptations are best accomplished by speaking with parents and caregivers and through being aware of any difficulties that may arise for the children during a program. Children who have physical impairments may have necessary equipment such as wheelchairs, special seating, or medical devices. It is important to plan for any adaptations that may be needed to accommodate any special equipment prior to the program. This information, which can be collected from the Special Needs Program Survey, will help you plan activities and spatial considerations, but if you are not aware of needs related to special equipment until the program begins, ask parents and caregivers what types of adaptations might help them attend the next session.

In addition to mobility impairments that may impact participation in programs, children may have other impairments that could potentially prevent them from participating in parts of your program. Visual and auditory impairments may prevent children from seeing or hearing some of the content of your program if you do not plan for necessary adaptations. When reading picture books during the whole-group portion of a program, use large books so children with visual impairments have less difficulty seeing the illustrations. When you read to the group, it is also helpful to walk through the room as you read, allowing each child to see the pages of the book up close. This approach is easier with a small group. Another option is to give copies of the book that you are reading to the children who have visual impairments. This way, children with visual impairments can look at their own copies of the book as you read the larger copy to the entire group.

For children with more severe visual impairments, several companies publish picture books in braille; however, purchasing braille books may not be within your library's collection budget. If this is the case, several companies offer grants for libraries, classrooms, and individuals who need braille books. In addition to braille books, you may want to consider tactile picture books. These books are created with 3-D printers, which your library may already own. The Tactile Picture Book Project (http://tpbp.wpengine.com/) offers free downloadable 3-D templates for creating several open source picture books. These printable books include raised pictures on each page as well as braille text that can be printed with a 3-D printer. You may choose to make these books available during your programs or you may even consider adding them to the collection for checkout.

Children who attend your program may also have auditory impairments that require adaptations to your program. Incorporating sign language into your program will help you communicate with children who are familiar with signing while exposing children who are not hearing impaired. There are many online resources that can help you learn simple signs, as well as community education courses, online webinars, and DVD resources. In addition to using sign language, speak clearly and make eye contact as much as possible for children who do not have a total hearing loss. Use facial expressions and gestures to help convey the meaning of the text. It is also important to encourage children who are hearing impaired to interact with other children through games and activities in order to foster social and language development. During music-based activities, the use of musical instruments that create vibrations and the incorporation of movement activities can help promote social inclusion of children with hearing impairments.

Reaching Out to Families with Children Who Have Special Needs

No matter a child's level of ability, your goal should be to offer an inclusive program that meets the individual needs of the children and families in attendance. Before you can serve these families in your programs, you will need to find them. If families with children who have special needs have not attended programs in the past, or if they are hesitant about attending programs, you will have to work to get them in the door of the library. This may prove difficult if they have not felt welcome in programs in the past. Reaching out to families through personal contact can help bring them in, but you may need to locate families before you can make that connection.

Collaborating with area schools can help you connect with families who do not attend programs at the library. Although schools cannot release confidential information concerning students, you may be able to work with the teachers and administrators in your community to send home information about upcoming library programs for children with special needs. You may be able to send Special Needs Program Surveys home with the students and request that the information be returned to the library—or provide information about accessing the survey online. In addition to reaching out to families through area schools, you may consider planning outreach programs to classrooms that serve children with special needs. Ask teachers about visiting their classrooms, and, before visiting, ask what types of needs the students might have. Field trips to the library may also be an option that could work well for some classrooms. Reach out to teachers and schools and let them know that you would like to offer programs and services to their students.

Workshops for parents and caregivers of children with special needs are another type of programming service that your library might consider. The Special Needs Program Survey (see the appendix) will help you discover the needs of parents and caregivers and the types of programs or speakers that would be most beneficial. Reach out to other community service providers that serve children with special needs and their families. Consider the ways that you might collaborate with these organizations to offer programs and workshops for parents and caregivers. When you use a whole-family and community approach, your programs for children with special needs are most likely to meet the needs of participants, which will help ensure program attendance and continued participation.

NOTES

1. Star Institute for Sensory Processing Disorder, "About SPD," https://www.spdstar.org/basic/about-spd.

2. Libraries and Autism, "This Is My Library," www.librariesandautism.org/new resources.htm.

3. Ashley Waring, "Sensory Storytime: A (Brief) How-To Guide," *ALSC Blog,* March 14, 2012, www.alsc.ala.org/blog/2012/03/sensory-storytime-a-brief-how-to-guide/.

4. Tzvi Schectman, "21 Great Fidgets for Your Child with Special Needs," *Friendship Circle* (blog), February 7, 2013, www.friendshipcircle.org/blog/2013/02/07/21-great-fidgets-for-your-child-with-special-needs/.

5. "Proprioception Explained," *Brain Balance* (blog), www.brainbalancecenters.com/blog/2015/08/proprioception-explained/.

6. Ilana Danneman, "Six Alternative Seating Options in the Classroom for a Child with Special Needs," *Friendship Circle* (blog), November 3, 2014, www.friendshipcircle.org/blog/2014/11/03/six-alternative-seating-arrangements-for-a-child-with-special-needs/.

7. Integrated Learning Strategies, "Why Weighted Lap Pads Are Used for Tactile Defensiveness and Sensory Integration," http://ilslearningcorner.com/2016-03-why-weighted-lap-pads-are-used-for-tactile-defensiveness-and-sensory-integration/.

8. National Institute of Mental Health, "Autism Spectrum Disorder," www.nimh.nih.gov/health/topics/autism-spectrum-disorders-asd/index.shtml.

9. U.S. Department of Justice, Civil Rights Division, "ADA Standards for Accessible Design," https://www.ada.gov/2010ADAstandards_index.htm.

9

Advocacy and Marketing Your K-5 Programs

NO MATTER HOW HARD YOU WORK ON PLANNING YOUR programs, without marketing and advocacy efforts, you won't reach the people who need to hear about your programs the most. Ask any library or community service organization, and staff members will likely tell you that the most difficult part of providing services to the community is finding the unserved. In order to reach more of your community, it is helpful to build collaborative partnerships with other community service organizations. Each partnership that you build can help you reach a population within the community that you may not otherwise reach. In turn, your library can support partner organizations through publicizing their services to your library's program participants. Such reciprocation creates a supportive partnership that offers your community the best information and services possible.

Advocacy Efforts

In addition to building collaborative partnerships, it is important that you advocate for library services among the community of services. This effort includes participation on local and state advisory boards and community councils. Placement on these committees provides a platform to share information about the services that are already provided by your library as well as the services that might be offered in the future. This exposure is especially helpful if you are seeking physical or financial support for upcoming library service projects. Participating on community councils allows you to seek support organically among other organizations while keeping the library's service plans transparent to the community. This transparency helps ensure an open line of communication that will help your library better identify needs in the community through creating an open dialogue.

In addition to community support, it is important to keep the library board informed of the needs of the community. As the first line of service to the public, you are the best connection between the community and the library board. When you use needs-based surveys or gather information in person from library participants, you need to share this information with the library board. This first-person information can be invaluable in helping you sell a needed program or service to the library board for funding approval. When presenting information to the board, whether it be in support of beginning a new program or continuing a previously offered program, it can be helpful to invite participants or potential participants to share a few words in support of the program. By providing the board with the best information from the most reliable sources possible, you are able to advocate for the programs that are most needed by the community that you serve.

In addition to advocating for your library's programs to other service organizations and the library board, it is important that you advocate for library programs to local and state policy makers. Doing so means being an active participant in applicable legislative and city council meetings. Be prepared to speak on behalf of the library by creating an "elevator speech," or a brief description of the programs and services that the library provides for children and families. This speech should be just a couple of minutes in length and should be in everyday language that does not rely heavily on library jargon that might be difficult for outsiders to understand. Use your prepared and practiced words to advocate for the library's services when presenting to policy makers and funders. Include brief, statistical information that quickly communicates the impact of the library's programs on the community or the needs for new programs based on already gathered information. Direct quotes from members of the community can be highlighted in this brief speech in order to provide evidence in support of specific programs for children. Not only does this personal evidence communicate the needs and interests of the community for library programs and services, but it also advocates for the relevance of overall public library services within the community. It has become increasingly important for libraries to provide evidence of their continued importance among other public services in the twenty-first century. Specific information needs to be shared that corroborates the necessity of public library programs that cannot be replaced by any other community institution. As those who advocate for the importance of literacy-based programs for children, we need also to advocate for the public library's relevance within our communities and states. We need to be sharing success stories and community needs in an effort to gain community-wide support and funding of library programs. Without these advocacy efforts, the public library is in danger of being considered less important within a community of services. It is up to us to advocate for our library's programs for children and the important role that they continue to play in building successful, lifelong readers in our communities.

Marketing and Promoting Your Programs

Your library's website is a natural place to promote and share information about your programs, but it is certainly not the only tool you should use. Effective marketing also reaches out into populations that may be unfamiliar with library programs and services. In order to reach these populations with information about your programs, you have to not only be aware of the places where they live but also establish a physical presence. Doing so is usually one of the most difficult parts of effective marketing because it is not easy to locate people that you have not been reaching. There are a few things that you can do to help with this process.

COMMUNITY PUBLIC SERVICE PARTNERSHIPS

Working with other community public service organizations is one way to discover the areas within your community where unserved or underserved families live. Although policies on confidentiality can prevent other organizations from passing along specific names or addresses, your library can provide informational materials to the organizations that are already providing services within these communities. These materials can include program calendars, flyers, or specially printed promotional items such as magnets, pencils, or bookmarks. You may also collaborate with other service organizations to cohost community programs in underserved areas. These outreach programs should bring information about your library's in-house programs directly to the people who live in the community while providing an example of library programming. Because your intent should be to help transition these families into library users, it is crucial that you provide a program that is similar to an in-house program. This strategy helps put unfamiliar families at ease about what programs are like. If transportation or financial issues prevent families from coming to the library, outreach programs may be the only ones that will work for them. It is important that outreach services continue to provide library programs for these families even after the initial outreach effort.

MEDIA

Another way to reach the community with your marketing efforts is through media outreach. Effective media outreach includes community newspapers, television, radio, and promotional media provided through other organizations. Media promotion can help you reach a variety of populations within your library's community, across socioeconomic and cultural segments. Be sure to take advantage of these types of media because they are usually free of charge and reach the widest audience of all the forms of marketing your library might try. Consider sending a press release about your programs to local news outlets. A press release should include contact information; information about your library; the intention of the event; the time, date, and location of the event; and any information about registration procedures (see the sample press release in the accompanying text box). A standard Press Release Template is available in the appendix to help you develop a press release for your library's program.

Local news programs will often share information about free local programs throughout the community, including library-sponsored programs. If your

Sample Press Release

FOR IMMEDIATE RELEASE

February 7, 2016

Tweens Battle of the Books Book Club

Cincinnati, OH—Students who are participating in the Battle of the Books intermediate book competition, join us at the library for a special book club and get a jump start on reading one of the books on the Battle list! When you register, come by the library and pick up a copy of the book that we will be discussing in the club over the course of three weeks. Participants will read the book on their own and return to discuss it with other participants during the three sessions scheduled at the library at 5:30 p.m. on Wednesday, February 23, Wednesday, March 2, and Wednesday, March 9. Registration is required and will begin on Monday, February 14. For more information, or to register, visit the library's website at www.mylibrary.com or contact the Youth Services Department at (502) 555-5555.

R. Lynn Baker
Youth Services Librarian
County Public Library
555 Main Street
Cincinnati, OH 45201
P (555)555-5555
name@mylibrary.org

community has a cable access channel, you may be able to advertise on community information boards or appear on community discussion-based forums that allow you to promote the library's programs for free. Local radio may also feature information about upcoming community events. Local media offer many opportunities to share information about your large events and community-wide library programs for children. If your community has a well-established newspaper, it is helpful to develop an ongoing relationship with the education reporters and photographers. Newspapers need stories on local events and will often offer free advertising on their community calendar of events. Photographs of community events also help newspapers communicate the things that are happening in the community. Newspapers may allow you to submit information and photos about programs, or news photographers may come to your programs to take photos for the paper. When you have an established relationship with the newspaper, reporters may even call the library from time to time asking if someone from the paper can attend library events and take photographs for the paper. Photos of library events in the newspaper show the community the types of programs that the library provides while promoting future programs and services as well.

In addition to the free advertising that local media provide, local television and radio stations will run paid commercial spots to promote your library's programs. Paid advertising such as this is usually reserved for large events or for programs that are costly for the library to provide. Billboards are another way that libraries can advertise large programs around the town or city where the library event will take place. Billboards are usually one of the most expensive ways of advertising an event, depending on their size, their location, and the length of time that the advertisement will be up on the billboard. For events (such as summer reading) that have more elaborate artwork, you can send the billboard company all the artwork, and the company will transfer the artwork onto the billboard. If your event does not have established artwork, many billboard companies can work with you to design a billboard with information about your event. Again, this type of advertisement is costly and is usually reserved for very large library events.

PRINTED MATERIALS

Flyers with information about upcoming programs can be designed and printed in-house and then distributed to patrons who come into the library. Flyers help promote programs to patrons whom you might see in the library regularly. Flyers can also be distributed through partner organizations and area schools. This approach can help you reach some families who do not usually attend programs at the library. Flyers can also be placed at various locations throughout the community that families are likely to visit, including pediatricians' offices, the health department, hospitals, family dental offices, hair salons, banks, or grocery stores. These places commonly have community bulletin boards in waiting areas where printed materials can be displayed for families. Community recreational centers, parks, and laundromats frequently offer bulletin boards where information can be pinned as well. Look for places in your community that families visit. Even if these places do not have bulletin boards, staff may allow you to post flyers in the window or may even be willing to distribute program information to their customers if you supply flyers.

Schools and after-school care providers may be willing to send home information about your programs if you are able to provide printed flyers. Offer to provide printed calendars or special event flyers as appropriate. For larger events, such as summer reading, consider asking to visit the school and speak directly with the children about upcoming programs. Coupled with flyers that go home with children, in-person presentations work well to excite children about your programs. Children are more likely to make an effort to show the library's flyer to their parents and ask to participate. You can couple printed flyers with incentive programs to help encourage children to visit the library as well. For example, you can distribute punch cards during your visit and encourage students to bring the punch cards with them each time they attend a library program. After obtaining a specified number of punches on the card, the student will receive a book or related reward. This promotional effort can be used to encourage program attendance and to let potential participants know about upcoming programs at the library.

BRANDING

In order to communicate your library's message about programming for children, it is important to create a market "brand" for your programs. Part of this brand should include your library's logo, location, and contact information. In addition to the library information, programs for specific ages should have their own image that is conveyed through your marketing materials. Any artwork or images that you choose to use for a specific program must be used in some form on all print and electronic materials that your library distributes. It is also helpful to use the same font or set of fonts for all text that appears on program materials and to include specific ages and registration information on all marketing materials. Creating consistent-looking materials for each age group helps communicate visually so that potential participants can easily recognize programs that are included on print materials. Print materials that are designed in this way create a form of program branding that can be used to grab the attention of people who are new to the library as well as returning patrons who are seeking information about specific programs.

In addition to creating consistent printed program materials, the registration process and program structure contribute to the branding of your programs. When registration is completed in a consistent manner with consistent steps and deadlines, you create a uniform design that helps make registration an easier process for participants. Making the process user-friendly means providing easy-to-follow instructions for new and repeat program registrants. When you make the process as easy and consistent as possible, you create a programming brand that encourages new participants to register for other programs in the future.

Although your programs may include fun activities that are intentionally planned to foster a love of reading and the development of language, social, and cognitive skills, without the proper attention to promoting your programs and advocating for them, you will not have anyone interested in attending them. Effective program planning is only half the equation. Promotional efforts are the other half. It is crucial that you are working to meet the programming needs of your community and then marketing your programs effectively to potential participants. In order to plan the best programs possible and to reach the highest number of the appropriate segment of the community, it is imperative that you advocate for the importance of your programs—among library policy makers, partners within the community, and, most important, potential families and participants.

Lesson Plans

LESSON PLANS FOR VARIOUS TYPES OF PROGRAMS ARE INCLUDED in this chapter. The lesson plans are divided into three sections— kindergarten through second grade, third through fifth grade, and all ages. Use the lesson plans as they are written, or adapt them to fit the needs of your library.

Lesson Plans for Kindergarten through Second Grade

Story-Based Program: Traditional Tales

WELCOME
Greet participants at the door or entrance to your program area. This courtesy helps put new participants at ease and provides consistency for repeat program participants. When all participants are seated, explain to the group that they will be hearing different versions of traditional fairy tales and that they will have the opportunity to help create a new fairy tale together.

ICEBREAKER GAME: FAIRY TALE CHARADES
Write the titles of different fairy tales or traditional stories on slips of paper. Ask each participant to draw a slip of paper and silently act out something from the fairy tale or story written on the slip. The rest of the group should guess what fairy tale is being acted out. The participant who guesses correctly should be the next person to act out the fairy tale or story on his slip of paper.

Repeat the process until all participants have had a chance to act out their fairy tales or stories.

Note: For younger children who have difficulty reading, you may provide an illustration or image of the fairy tale or story to be portrayed or provide assistance with reading the slip of paper very quietly so that the rest of the group does not overhear.

SUGGESTED FAIRY TALES
"The Three Little Pigs"
"Little Red Riding Hood"
"Cinderella"
"Jack and the Beanstalk"
"Goldilocks and the Three Bears"
"Rapunzel"
"Sleeping Beauty"
"The Princess and the Pea"
"The Tortoise and the Hare"
"Pinocchio"

INFORMATION FOR PARTICIPANTS
Explain to the children that you will be reading two versions of "The Three Little Pigs" next. Encourage participants to pay attention to the similarities and differences in each version of the story.

BOOK
The Three Little Pigs by Paul Galdone (HMH Books for Young Readers, 1984)

INFORMATION FOR PARTICIPANTS
Explain to the group that the next version of "The Three Little Pigs" changes some parts to make the story funny. Explain that this type of story is called a *parody*. Explain that participants should listen for the parts of the story that are different from the first book that was read and try to remember the differences for a discussion when you are finished reading the entire book.

BOOK
The True Story of the Three Little Pigs by Jon Scieszka (Puffin Books, 1996)

WHOLE-GROUP ACTIVITY: SIMILARITIES AND DIFFERENCES
Ask participants to help identify the parts of each book that are similar and the parts that differ. Create a chart on large paper or a wipe-off board to help

participants visualize the similarities and differences between the two books. Fill in two columns (labeled *Same* and *Different*) with pictures or words that signify the parts of the story that fall under each category. Discuss as a group whether the stories are more alike or different. Tally the number of differences and similarities to help the group decide how similar or different the two stories are.

INFORMATION FOR PARTICIPANTS

Introduce the next fairy tale, "Jack and the Beanstalk." Explain to the group that the book that you are going to read is a retelling of a story that has been told as far back as the sixteenth century. Explain that fairy tales were first told orally and that when traditional fairy tales are rewritten by new authors, the result is said to be a *retelling* of the story. Explain that you will all work together to create a retelling of the story after reading the book.

BOOK

Jack and the Beanstalk by E. Nesbit (Candlewick, 2006)
Note: As an alternative to reading the book, you may choose to share this story through storytelling by committing the text to memory.

INTERACTIVE ACTIVITY

Ask the group to help develop a retelling or a parody of "Jack and the Beanstalk." Write down the new story in the exact words of the participants. If you have adults in the room, you may consider splitting the whole group into smaller groups and assigning different parts of the story for each group to rewrite. Ask participants to create illustrations to support the written text. When the retelling and illustrations are complete, bind the pages together and make the completed book available for checkout.

Play-Based Program: Games from Around the World

WELCOME AND INTRODUCTION

Welcome participants and explain how each of the interactive stations is meant to work. Explain the procedure for choosing the first activity as well as the procedure for moving from activity to activity. If you will be signaling participants by ringing a bell, playing music, or dimming lights when it is time to move to the next station, be sure to explain what signal you will be using and which station is next in the rotation.

Explain that most children play games, no matter where they live. This program will allow children to participate in games that children from different countries and cultures enjoy. Before the children begin working at the stations, go around the room and give the whole group information about each country and activity represented.

Note: Place instructions and table tents with the name of the game at each table prior to the program.

ACTIVITY STATIONS

1. *Malaysia: Wan, Tu, Zum* (similar to Rock, Paper, Scissors):[1] Explain to participants that the Malaysian culture has been influenced by a combination of traditions from China, India, and many other cultures. Explain that this game can be played across cultures and languages because it involves symbols made with the hands. To play the game, two participants stand or sit facing each other. Each participant claps one fist into the other open hand as both participants say, "Bird, Rock, Plank, Water." Then participants each choose one of the signs to make with their hands:

   » Bird (beats plank and water): Participant makes one hand into a beak by holding all fingertips of one hand together.
   » Rock (beats bird and plank): Participant makes a fist with one hand.
   » Plank (beats bird and water): Participant stretches one hand open, palm down, with all fingers together.
   » Water (beats rock): Participant holds one hand palm up with all fingers together.

2. *Trinidad: Trier:*[2] Explain to participants that Trinidad is part of an island nation called Trinidad and Tobago. Explain that the island is considered part of South America and the Caribbean. The culture is made up of East Indian, African, and Venezuelan traditions. To play the game, participants place five small, dried beans on the back of one hand. Each participant tosses the beans into the air and tries to catch them with the same hand. The participant repeats the process until she catches all five beans.

3. *Penobscot Native American: Wiigwaas Ball and Triangle Game:*[3] Explain to participants that the ball and triangle game is a traditional game played by Native American children. The game was originally made from birch tree bark. Explain that birch bark was vitally important to the Penobscot Native Americans in northeastern Maine because the people made

many things with it, including canoes and toys. To make the game, pre-cut four-inch-high cardboard triangles. Precut a hole in the center of each triangle. Encourage children to decorate their cardboard triangles using markers. Provide a small stone for each child to use as the "ball" for the toy. Provide string for attaching the stone ball to the triangle. Punch a small hole through one corner of the triangle for children to attach one end of the string and then tie the other end around the stone ball. Encourage the children to swing their triangle, attempting to make the stone ball go through the hole in the middle of the triangle.

4. *Mexico: Miniature Pull-String Piñatas:*[4] Explain to participants that piña-tas began in China but made their way to Mexico, where the more mod-ernized version of the piñata was first developed. Explain that in Mex-ico, large piñatas are usually made from papier-mâché, or glue-covered tissue paper, and filled with candy, fruit, and nuts. Explain that partic-ipants usually swing a stick at the piñata while blindfolded, trying to break the piñata to release the goodies inside. Explain that the piñatas that participants will make will have a ribbon to pull that will release the goodies when they use their piñatas at home. Provide plain, colored birthday party hats for the piñata form. Encourage children to decorate their party hat form with crayons, markers, and stickers. Provide small toys and candy for the children to fill their birthday hat–shaped piñatas and tissue paper to cover the open end of the hat. Encourage children to tape a piece of ribbon to the tissue paper. Pulling this piece of ribbon will release the treats inside the piñata.

CLOSING THE PROGRAM

It is especially important to provide a countdown as your program approaches the end of the allotted time. This reminder helps children transition and gives them time to wrap up their own activities. Distribute information regarding upcoming programs, and consider distributing surveys for participants to express interest in other programs for the future.

STEAM (Science, Technology, Engineering, Art, Math) Program: Building Structures

STEAM activities should provide participants the opportunity to engage in hands-on exploration and experimental activities that lead to the discovery of new ideas and concepts.

WELCOME AND INTRODUCTION

Greet participants and have everyone take a seat together at the front of the room. (Have materials arranged in the back of the room at interactive stations.) Explain that participants will be using science, technology, engineering, art, and math to build various structures that can stand on their own.

INFORMATION FOR PARTICIPANTS

Introduce the book and explain that this is the story of Iggy Peck, a boy who builds creations using all kinds of different materials.

BOOK

Iggy Peck, Architect by Andrea Beaty; illustrated by David Roberts (Abrams Books for Young Readers, 2007)

INFORMATION FOR PARTICIPANTS

Discuss all the different types of materials that Iggy Peck used and why each type of material would work or not work to create a building. Discuss the different types of materials that are used to build real buildings. Explain that there are various materials in the back of the room that participants can use to build their own buildings. Explain that the only rule is that their structures must be able to stand on their own. Before participants begin building with the materials, give the entire group a brief tour of the stations, offering information about each item on the tables. Encourage participants to try various combinations of the items to build their own structures that can stand completely on their own.

BUILDING MATERIALS
- Wooden craft sticks
- Toothpicks
- Gumdrops
- Dry, uncooked spaghetti noodles
- Miniature marshmallows

- Dry, uncooked wagon wheel noodles
- Plastic coffee stirrers or small straws
- Plastic cups (various sizes—party size, medicine size, bathroom size)
- Pipe cleaners
- Playdough
- Liquid glue or tape
- Measuring tape or ruler

CLOSING THE PROGRAM

It is especially important to provide a countdown as your program approaches the end of the allotted time. About ten minutes before the end, ask the participants to take turns telling the group about their completed structures. Encourage children to share the steps in their building procedure, including choosing materials, figuring out which things worked and which didn't work, and any methods used to measure and fit items together.

Craft Club: Paper Crafts

The craft club can meet once a week, once every two weeks, or once a month, depending on the needs of your library. A paper craft club can introduce different types of paper crafts during each session, including card making, painting, origami or paper folding, drawing, stamping, and any other crafts that use paper. This program will feature torn-paper mosaics.

PREPARING ACTIVITY MATERIALS

Provide pencils and white card stock so children can draw pictures that they will fill in with torn pieces of patterned paper. Supply various colors and patterns of scrapbook paper to be torn. Children will tear pieces of patterned paper to fill in their drawings and then glue the pieces down using a glue stick. You may also want to have scissors readily available for children who wish to cut pieces of the scrapbook paper rather than, or in addition to, tearing the paper.

CHOOSING BOOKS

Before the program, select books to display for checkout. The books that you choose for display should have examples of paper crafts that are similar to the projects you are offering during your program. You may also want to make these books available for use during your program, especially if the books provide ideas, break down steps, or offer craft expansion ideas.

WELCOME AND INTRODUCTION

Welcome participants to the program and explain that a different paper craft will be introduced each week. Explain to the participants that for this week's program they will be creating torn-paper mosaics.

INFORMATION FOR PARTICIPANTS

Explain to participants that a mosaic is a picture made up of small, colored pieces. Explain to the participants that they will create a mosaic by drawing a picture and then filling in the parts of the picture with small pieces of torn colored paper. This process will create a picture that is similar in appearance to a pieced quilt.

CLOSING THE PROGRAM

It is important to give the children a countdown as they are working so that they have time to complete their mosaic projects and clean their areas before the close of the program. Because glue sticks are used for adhering the pieces of patterned paper, participants will not have to wait for their creations to dry before leaving with their completed projects.

AFTER THE PROGRAM: DISPLAY

Participants can share their completed mosaics with the entire group at the close of the program, or, if wall space is available at the library, consider creating a gallery of completed mosaics for patrons to view after the program.

Gaming Program: Social Games

WELCOME AND INTRODUCTION

Welcome participants and explain how each of the interactive stations is meant to work. Explain the procedure for choosing the first activity as well as the procedure for moving from activity to activity. If you will be signaling participants by ringing a bell, playing music, or dimming lights when it is time to move to the next station, be sure to explain what signal you will be using and which station is next in the rotation. Before participants choose their first stations, provide a brief tour of each station with instructions on how to play the games.

ACTIVITY STATIONS

1. *Guessing Game:* Provide two cardboard headbands with one side of a piece of Velcro positioned on the front. Two players will play the game

together. Print out two stacks of ten four-by-six-inch cards with different images. Place a piece of the other side of the Velcro on the back of each image card. Ten cards should be placed facedown in front of each player. Players will take turns choosing a card from the top of their pile and placing it (without looking at it) on their headband. The other player should describe the image on the headband without naming the object. The player with the image should guess what the object is by listening to the other player's description. Players continue to take turns describing and guessing objects on their cards until they have gone through all the cards in both stacks.

2. *Old-Fashioned Games:* Provide an old-fashioned game or two, such as jacks, pick-up sticks, and tiddlywinks. Be sure to provide instructions verbally and printed on a table tent at each table or in each area for playing the game. Encourage children to work together to play each of the games you provide.

3. *Board Games, Card Games, and Paper Games:* Provide simple games for participants to play together, such as checkers, dominoes, Go Fish, card matching and memory games, tic-tac-toe, and dots and boxes.[5] Provide paper and pencils for playing paper games. Keeping score at this age is not important. The goal of these games should be to help children learn the rules and how to work with peers socially. Problem solving is an important skill that is fostered through each of these games.

4. *Thinking Games:* Thinking games offer participants the opportunity to solve problems, and many foster spatial reasoning skills. At this station, offer activities such as tangrams, tangle puzzles, and sliding puzzles. Tangram puzzles are seven-piece, geometric-shape puzzles that originated in China.[6] The seven pieces fit together to form a large square and can be arranged in different patterns to create outlines of different shapes. Tangrams and tangram patterns can be printed from various online sites, and three-dimensional tangrams can be purchased from educational supply stores. The individual pieces should be placed end-to-end without overlapping to create a whole image. Encourage participants to create tangram images to match patterns that you print on card stock prior to the program. Tangle puzzles can be purchased from educational supply stores.[7] These puzzles are made from plastic or metal and include at least two pieces that are twisted together. The object of the tangle puzzle is to untangle the pieces and pull them apart. Sliding puzzles are usually small, plastic, flat puzzles that have fifteen

sliding pieces inside a frame. The pieces may have numerals printed on them that need to be put in order, or they may have parts of an image that have to be slid into the correct order to make a complete image.

CLOSING THE PROGRAM

It is especially important to provide a countdown as your program approaches the end of the allotted time. This reminder helps children transition and gives them the opportunity to wrap up their own activities. Distribute information regarding upcoming programs, and consider distributing surveys for participants to express interest in other programs for the future.

Lesson Plans for Third through Fifth Grades

Readers' Theater Program: Stellaluna (Multiple Sessions)

BOOK

Stellaluna by Janell Cannon (Houghton Mifflin Harcourt, 1993). This picture book tells the story of a baby bat who loses her mother and finds her way to a nest of baby birds. Stellaluna stays with the birds, trying to live as they do, but she notices that there are many differences between them. Eventually, Stellaluna discovers that she is really a bat and is reunited with her mother, but she also discovers that she can still be friends with the birds who are different from her.

PROPS TO PREPARE

- Sets of wings for each bird: Bat wings can be made from trash bags or a plastic tablecloth. Bird wings can be made from cardboard and feathers.
- Bat ears: Create small ears from card stock or stiff felt and attach them to plastic headbands.
- Tree branches for the background: Place large branches in plant stands.
- Owl mask and wings: Glue brown feathers to a paper mask purchased from a craft store. Owl wings can be made by attaching brown feathers to the arms of a brown sweatshirt.
- Bird nest: Fill a baby pool with straw to create a nest for the baby birds.
- Bird beaks: Create beaks for each of the birds using card stock. Attach yarn or elastic so the participants can put on the beaks like masks.
- Plastic toy grasshoppers, worms, or other insects for the birds to eat.

- A mango for Stellaluna to eat (can be plastic or real).
- Light dimmer and two backdrops to convey night and day (dark and light).

PARTS AND PARTICIPANTS

Backstage
- Stage Director: This person will assist with practices and help keep participants on task during rehearsals.
- Costume Design: These people will create simple costumes for readers in the performance.
- Props and Staging: These people will help move props in and out as needed and will be in charge of moving any furniture on the set during the performance.
- Lighting and Sound: These people will be in charge of lighting and adjusting the sound levels during the performance (if applicable to your performance site).

Reading or Performing Parts
- Narrator: This person will read the story line and should be a strong reader. You may choose to have the story read straight from the text of the book, or you may choose to rewrite the parts to shorten the story or better convey what is happening in the story.
- Mother Bat: This person will portray Stellaluna's mother, who drops Stellaluna when an owl swoops after her.
- Owl: This person will fly after Stellaluna and her mother, swooping around them.
- Stellaluna: This is the lead part. This person should have strong acting skills and the ability to physically act out the story as the narrator reads the storyline. This person should also be a strong reader.
- Flap, Flitter, and Pip: Three baby birds in a nest.
- Mama Bird: This person will be chased by the owl while holding on to the person who is playing Stellaluna. This person is included at the beginning of the performance and does not appear again until the end of the performance.
- The bat that finds Stellaluna: This person will portray the bat that happens upon Stellaluna as she is hanging the wrong way from a tree limb.
- A small group of bats (three or four people): These people will be dressed like bats and will "hang" upside down on a branch.
  - » *Note:* To create the illusion that bats are hanging upside down, use chairs with branches on them for participants to sit in upside down.

PROGRAM SESSION SEQUENCE

Week 1: During the first session, distribute the scripts and read through the entire script together as a group. This reading will give participants an idea of the parts that are included and give them time to consider what parts they may be interested in reading for the performance. Ask participants to come to the next session with their top three choices. Allow participants to take copies of the scripts home to practice. Keep the original scripts in folders at the library between practice sessions. This precaution will ensure that original scripts are not lost and are available for every practice.

Week 2: Ask participants to bring their scripts with them, along with their top three choices for roles (reading or backstage). Run through the script a few times, allowing participants to read for the various parts they are interested in. You may choose to use this session as a tryout for parts, using the observations you make from the readings but also considering the top three choices that the participants bring with them. Assign parts and backstage positions after the session and inform participants by posting a list, by texting or e-mailing, or by calling. You may need to adjust the number of parts you have in your script, based on the number of reading participants that you have in your group. You will need to decide what needs to be added or removed from your script as you assign parts and backstage positions.

Week 3: Participants who are costume designers need to begin working on the costumes and props this week. Wings, feathers, masks, and ears need to be made during this session. While the costume design is taking place, the prop and staging participants can begin working on backdrops and creating the trees and nest. The stage director needs to run through the script and movements with the participants while props and backdrops are being made. During this and the following three sessions, the library should be marketing and promoting the upcoming performance to the public, including any registration procedures that may be in place. Remind participants that practice and attendance are important in order for the performance to be successful.

Week 4: The stage director should run through the script with all participants and any props and pieces of costumes that are ready. Make adjustments to props, backdrops, and costumes as needed. Encourage participants to read with expression, and make plans for the dress rehearsal to take place during the next session. Costume and backdrop designers should spend this session wrapping up their work as much as possible. Minor adjustments can be made during the dress rehearsal, but the majority of the work should be complete prior to the next session. If possible, allow the lighting and sound people to run through their roles as the readers practice.

Week 5: Use this session as a dress rehearsal with all costumes, props, scene changes, and backdrops. If possible, allow the lighting and sound crew to run through all procedures in real time as the readers perform the entire script. Make any last-minute adjustments to the props, costumes, or staging. Run through the script as many times as possible to make certain all participants are comfortable with their lines and duties. Ask participants to arrive one hour before the performance at the next session. This early arrival will ensure plenty of time for running through the script one last time and double-checking all costumes, props, and the set prior to the performance. The library should create and print simple programs for the audience at the final performance.

Week 6: Because participants will arrive early before the performance, they should help set up the room, stage area, and props. The stage director should read through the script with the readers one time without props or full stage movements. Participants should get dressed in costume. The sound and lighting should be checked to make sure they are in working order. The director, costume designers, and those working on props and staging should act as greeters at the entrance. They may also hand out programs and show people to their seats before the performance. Just before the performance, announce the book title and author and briefly summarize how the story begins.

AFTER THE PROGRAM

Consider having an after-performance party for participants and their families to reward them for their hard work.

Club Program: Gaming Club (Multiple Sessions)

Choose a different computer game or gaming system as the focus of each session. Depending on your choice for each session, decide whether participants will need to bring their own gaming equipment or whether you will offer the session in the library's computer lab.

PROGRAM SESSION SEQUENCE

Session 1: Computers—If your library has a computer lab with multiple computers, consider offering interactive games that allow participants to play online with one another. Subscriptions to online games allow many players to play the same game at one time. Subscription games include sandbox-style games in which participants can build their own worlds and creations within the game.[8] Players can play together, alone, or against one another. Open-world games are another type of subscription game that many people can play together. These games offer exploration of various worlds that already exist within the game, and there are generally no barriers that players need to pass to move from one section of the game to another.[9] Examples of games of this type that tweens might be interested in playing with others in a program include Minecraft, car/train/plane simulator games, or community simulation games, such as Animal Crossing. Consider polling your patrons to find out what they are most interested in. Work with your library's IT department to find out what is needed for tweens to play one of these types of games on computers in the library's lab. Some games, such as Minecraft, require that you install the game on each computer and then you are able to set up a server for participants to access together.

Session 2: Handheld Personal Gaming Systems—In this session, participants can bring their own handheld personal gaming systems and play together through the library's wireless Internet access. Poll possible participants ahead of time to discover what personal gaming systems are most popular. You may choose to host a program focused on specific games that are played on those personal gaming systems, such as Pokémon games, or you can host a free-choice program but specify the type of gaming system to ensure that players are able to play games with other participants.

Session 3: Gaming Consoles—In this session, participants will play together using a singular gaming system that is owned by the library and displayed through one common source, such as a projector. This program can be similar to a tournament, in which players play against other players in the same bracket. If your library has a large enough space and access to multiple monitors, you may also consider making various consoles available at once if your library owns more than one type. You may also want to offer snacks and other activities, such as board or card games, for participants to play as they wait to play in their round.

Session 4: Tablets or Smartphones—In this session, you may choose to make tablets available if your library owns enough for multiple players or to require participants to bring their own tablets or phones in order to attend. This program can be organized around a specific game that participants already have installed and know how to play, or you can combine this session with teaching participants how to play a game that they may have not yet learned. Location-based reality games, such as Pokémon Go, can be taught during a program. Participants can then all go out and play it together, or the program can focus solely on teaching participants how to play the game.

DISPLAY BOOKS AND MATERIALS

Take the opportunity to display books, video games, DVDs, and other materials that relate to gaming. Encourage participants to check out display titles to learn more about each type of game that you feature in this program series.

CLOSING THE PROGRAM

It is particularly helpful in a gaming program, in which participants are fully engaged in play, to give updates on the amount of time that remains. It is also helpful to make timers available to ensure that all participants who wish to have a turn are able to have a turn, particularly in console tournament-style programs. At the close of the program, be sure to distribute surveys to ask for input on other gaming programs, and provide information about the next session or other upcoming programs that may be of interest to participants.

STEAM (Science, Technology, Engineering, Art, Math) Program: Grab Bag Contraptions

Choose items to place in one medium-sized paper bag for each child. The bags should include various items that can be put together to build part of a contraption similar to a Rube Goldberg machine (see https://www.rubegoldberg.com/). Because of the complexity of this program, consider extending the time to an hour and a half or splitting the program into two sessions.

WELCOME AND INTRODUCTION

Welcome participants and ask them to have a seat at the table until all participants are seated. Explain to the participants that they will be creating a contraption together. Explain that a contraption is an invention that uses several complex motions that work together to complete one simple task. Explain how contraptions were inspired by Rube Goldberg's weekly cartoons, which portrayed complicated inventions with several steps for completing simple activities. Show the group a video of a contraption to give them a better idea of how one works. Several can be found on the Rube Goldberg website.[10]

BAGS

Ask participants to choose a bag. Explain that each person will contribute to the creation of one large contraption. Each bag includes items that can be used together to create one part of the contraption and that can be added to the items in other bags to extend the contraption. Explain to the participants that they will need to decide what the result of the contraption will be before they begin working on each piece. Offer guidance as the group works together to create their plans and the final contraption.

MATERIAL SUGGESTIONS FOR BAGS

- Ping-Pong balls
- Paper clips
- Rubber bands
- Small plastic or paper cups
- Marbles
- Small, metal springs
- Clothespins
- Matchbox car tracks or wooden train tracks
- String, yarn, or twine
- Rubber balls
- Small pulley wheels (can be purchased at the craft store)
- Small pieces of PVC pipe and elbow connector pieces
- Dominoes
- Binder clips
- Straws
- Matchbox cars
- Paper towel tubes
- Tennis balls
- Wooden rulers
- Wooden craft sticks

CLOSING THE PROGRAM

It is especially important to announce how much time remains in this program because participants must be able to complete their activities in order for the final product to work. Give a countdown of the time as you approach the end of the program. Provide handouts about contraption activities that participants can try at home, along with information about other upcoming STEAM-based programs.

Lesson Plans for All Ages

Story-Based Family or Multigenerational Program: Let's Be Silly

Programs that are planned for entire families should include activities that are appropriate for all ages. Family programs should be intentionally planned to encourage the participation of all members of the family. When planning family programs, it is important to remember that these programs are multigenerational. The goal of a multigenerational program should always be to connect all members of the family and inspire interaction through literacy-based activities.

WELCOME AND INTRODUCTION

Welcome families at the door. Have quiet items (for example, squeezable toys, pipe cleaners, stretchy toys, or plastic spring toys) in a basket for younger children who may need to fidget during the program. Have space available on the floor for children and caregivers to sit, but also make chairs available for those who may not be able to sit on the floor.

INFORMATION FOR PARTICIPANTS

Explain to participants that the program will include lots of silly stories and activities. Explain that you will read stories and do some activities together and then there will be interactive stations with activities for families to do together during the second half of the program.

SONG

"Hello, Neighbor!"[11] (to the tune of "Good Night, Ladies")
Hello, neighbor. (*wave*)
What do you say? (*high five*)
It's going to be a happy day. (*slap your legs, clap your hands, slap hands with your neighbor*)
Greet your neighbor. (*shake your neighbor's hand*)
Boogie on down. (*wiggle down to the floor*)
Give a bump, (*bump your hips with a neighbor*)
And then sit down. (*sit on the floor or chair*)

BOOK

Silly Sally by Audrey Wood (HMH Books for Young Readers, 1999)

GAME

"Ha, Ha, Ha!"
This game moves around from person to person in the room. The first person says "Ha," the second person says, "Ha, ha," the third person says "Ha, ha, ha," and so on. An adult can participate for a younger child if necessary.

BOOK

A Boy and His Bunny by Sean Bryan (Arcade Publishing, 2011)

SONG

"Herman the Worm"[12]

I was sittin' on a fencepost, chewing my bubblegum
(chew, chew, chew, chew)
Playin' with my yo-yo, (doo-wop, doo-wop)
When along came Herman the Worm,
And he was this big, (*bring out small worm*)
And I said, "Herman, what happened?"
And he said, "I ate a _____." (ewwwwww)
The next day . . .

(Repeat through all worm sizes, until you go back to the smallest at the end.)

I was sittin' on a fencepost, chewing my bubblegum
(chew, chew, chew, chew)
Playin' with my yo-yo, (doo-wop, doo-wop)
When along came Herman the Worm,
And he was this big, (*bring out small worm*)
And I said, "Herman, what happened?"
And he said, "I burped. Excuse me."

BOOK

Is Everyone Ready for Fun? by Jan Thomas (Beach Lane Books, 2011)

SONG

"A-Root-Chy-Cha Chant"
(*Participants echo and copy motions*)

Hands up! (*put hands up in the air*)
Wrists together! (*put wrists together*)
Chorus: A-root-chy-cha, a-root-chy-cha, a-root-chy-cha CHA!
A-root-chy-cha, a-root-chy-cha, a-root-chy-cha CHA!

Hands up! (*put hands up in the air*)
Wrists together! (*put wrists together*)
Elbows in! (*put elbows together*)
Chorus: A-root-chy-cha, a-root-chy-cha, a-root-chy-cha CHA!
A-root-chy-cha, a-root-chy-cha, a-root-chy-cha CHA!

Hands up! (*put hands up in the air*)
Wrists together! (*put wrists together*)
Elbows in! (*put elbows together*)
Head back! (*tilt head back*)
Chorus: A-root-chy-cha, a-root-chy-cha, a-root-chy-cha CHA!
A-root-chy-cha, a-root-chy-cha, a-root-chy-cha CHA!

(*Keep going back to the beginning, adding one motion each time.*)

Add: Knees together . . . Toes together . . . Bottom out . . . Eyes closed . . . Tongue out . . . Turn around . . . Sit down

INTERACTIVE STATIONS

Include table tents with instructions for families to engage in each of the activities at the various interactive stations.

- *Station 1—Silly Sentences:* Print various words on index cards, including common verbs (*are, is, were,* etc.) and nouns (people, places, and things). Encourage participants to place word cards on the table to create silly sentences.
- *Station 2—Silly Art:* Provide various nontraditional items and suggestions for participants to paint with on paper to create a silly masterpiece. Suggested items for use as "paintbrushes" might include feathers, buttons, matchbox cars, corks, clothespins, bubble wands, spoons, forks, bath puffs, backscratchers, or other items. Also suggest using different body parts as paintbrushes, such as elbows, chins, noses, or wrists.

- *Station 3—Tongue Twisters:* Provide printed tongue twisters for adults to try to teach to their children and vice versa. Add a few to the following list or trade some out, depending on the age and speech abilities of your participants.

  » "Peter Piper picked a peck of pickled peppers.
  » If Peter Piper picked a peck of pickled peppers,
  » How many pickled peppers did Peter Piper pick?"
  » Repeat three times: "Rubber baby buggy bumper."
  » "She sells seashells by the seashore."
  » "The cook took a good look at the cookbook."
  » "Toy boat. Toy boat. Toy boat."
  » "Six slippery snails slid slowly seaward."
  » Repeat three times: "Unique New York."
  » "Swan swam over the sea,
  » Swim, swan, swim!
  » Swan swam back again.
  » Well swum, swan!"
  » "Patty plays patty cake."
  » "Pass the pickles please, Paul."

- *Station 4—Keep Your Feather in the Air:* Provide colorful craft feathers. Encourage one member of each family to blow a feather, trying to keep it up in the air while the rest of the family sings "Twinkle, Twinkle, Little Star." If the feather falls, the next person tries to keep the feather in the air while the rest sing.

CLOSING THE PROGRAM

As participants work at the interactive stations, announce the time that remains prior to the end of the program (at fifteen, ten, and five minutes). These reminders will help participants prepare for the transition and manage their time as they complete each of the activity stations. At the close of the program, meet participants at the door and distribute information about other upcoming family programs.

Quiet Sensory Program for Children with Special Needs: Feelings

This program should be appropriate for children with sensory integration issues and children who may be on the autism spectrum. Lighting should be low, and any music should be soft and played at low volume. Display a program time line at the front of the room with images that represent each part of the program. As you move through each activity, remove the image that matches that activity. This technique helps children transition from activity to activity.

WELCOME AND INTRODUCTION
After children and families enter the room, offer small toys for children who may need to fidget. Allow children who may need special items from home to bring those items into the room to help them feel comfortable in their surroundings.

INFORMATION FOR PARTICIPANTS
Explain to adult participants that the activities in this session were chosen to help foster the children's ability to recognize the emotions of others.

SONG
"Hello, How Are You?" (to the tune of "Skip to My Lou")

> Hello, how are you?
> Hello, how are you?
> Hello, how are you?
> How are you today?

BOOK
My Many Colored Days by Dr. Seuss (Knopf Books for Young Readers, 1996)

RHYME
"I Look in the Mirror"
Give out pieces of reflective silver posterboard for children to use as mirrors as you recite this rhyme. Encourage children and adults to make faces that match each of the emotions that are identified in the rhyme.

> I look in the mirror, and what do I see?
> I see a happy face smiling at me.

> I look in the mirror and what do I see?
> I see a surprised face looking at me.

I look in the mirror and what do I see?
I see a sad face looking at me.

I look in the mirror and what do I see?
I see a shy face looking at me.

I look in the mirror and what do I see?
I see a scared face looking at me.

I look in the mirror and what do I see?
I see a mad face looking at me.

I look in the mirror and what do I see?
I see a happy face looking at me.

BOOK

Lots of Feelings by Shelley Rotner (Millbrook Press, 2003)

INTERACTIVE SONG

"If You're Happy/Mad/Excited/Sad and You Know It"
Prepare two large wooden craft sticks for each child. One stick should have clip art of a happy face on one side and a mad face on the other side. The other stick should have clip art of an excited face on one side and a sad face on the other. Encourage children to choose the appropriate sides of the sticks as you sing the song.

If you're happy and you know it, share a smile.
If you're happy and you know it, share a smile.
If you're happy and you know it, then your face will surely show it.
If you're happy and you know it, share a smile.

If you're mad and you know it, share a scowl.
If you're mad and you know it, share a scowl.
If you're mad and you know it, then your face will surely show it.
If you're mad and you know it, share a scowl.

If you're excited and you know it, show it now.
If you're excited and you know it, show it now.
If you're excited and you know it, then your face will surely show it.
If you're excited and you know it, show it now.

If you're sad and you know it, shed a tear.
If you're sad and you know it, shed a tear.
If you're sad and you know it, then your face will surely show it.
If you're sad and you know it, shed a tear.

If you're happy and you know it, share a smile.

If you're happy and you know it, share a smile.

If you're happy and you know it, then your face will surely show it.

If you're happy and you know it, share a smile.

FELT OR MAGNET BOARD: HOW DOES IT FEEL?

Prepare several cutout felt faces with matching emotions for each of the stories. Ask children to hold the felt pieces and place the appropriate face on the board when the story that you tell matches that emotion. Make several faces of each emotion to ensure that every child gets an opportunity to participate.

- *Story 1—Happy*: Jenny drew a picture for her grandma and took it to her when she went to visit. Her grandma loved the picture that Jenny drew and hung it up on her refrigerator. How do you think Jenny feels?
- *Story 2—Sad*: Zach lost his favorite toy truck. He looked for it everywhere, but couldn't find it. How do you think Zach feels?
- *Story 3—Shy*: Jackson is playing at the park when David comes up and asks his name. David wants to know if Jackson wants to play. Jackson has never met David before. How do you think Jackson feels?
- *Story 4—Excited*: Tomorrow is Kelsey's birthday. She is going to have a party at her house with her friends. How do you think Kelsey feels?
- *Story 5—Scared*: José was walking across the room to get his shoes. José jumped when he looked down and almost stepped on a spider. How do you think José was feeling?
- *Story 6—Mad*: Emma's sister took her crayon while she was coloring and ran across the room with it. How do you think that made Emma feel?

INFORMATION FOR PARTICIPANTS

Explain to participants that you are going to sing a goodbye song together and that participants can then spend time creating feelings collages on their own. If there are children who need to leave at this point, that is fine. Offer the collage activity for those who are interested in participating, but explain that the activity is completely optional.

CLOSING SONG

"Goodbye, We'll See You Soon" (to the tune of "Skip to My Lou")

Goodbye, we'll see you soon.

Goodbye, we'll see you soon.

Goodbye, we'll see you soon.

See you all next time.

SENSORY ACTIVITY: FEELINGS COLLAGES

Place clear contact paper on tables or on a floor tray for those who need to sit on the floor. Supply many different types of materials for the collage (such as yarn, jiggle eyes, buttons, feathers, tissue paper, sequins, paper and punches, wooden craft sticks, pom-poms, etc.). Encourage children to make collages to show how they are feeling. Children may choose to make face outlines with the yarn and then fill in items to create faces, or they may choose to make a random collage to convey their feelings.

Pop-Up/Impromptu Program: Favorite Genre Book Club

Decorate six small plastic tubs (recycled margarine tubs work well). Label each tub with a different genre: historical fiction, adventure, nonfiction, humor, graphic novels, biographies. Place colorful pom-poms, buttons, or paper clips in a basket near the tubs. Create a sign that encourages patrons to place one of the chosen objects in the corresponding tub to cast a vote for their favorite genre. On the sign, explain how many times each person is allowed to vote and how often. Also include the deadline for casting votes. At the conclusion of the voting, use the results to offer a book club in the winning genre.

BOOK CLUB

If it is within your library's budget, order copies of the chosen book for each participant to pick up one week prior to the club's first session. Based on the length of the book, you may choose to offer only one session or spread out the book club over two to four sessions. To help you order the appropriate number of books, you will want to offer preregistration and set a maximum number of participants.

BOOK CLUB ACTIVITIES

Base planned activities on the content of the chosen book. Try to include at least one hands-on activity that connects directly to the plot, characters, cultural traditions, or interests of the characters in the book.

ALTERNATIVES

You may choose to offer the book club to tweens only, or you may choose to open the club to tweens and their parents and caregivers. This decision can be based on the book and interest level.

OUTCOMES

This type of impromptu program that leads to an active program can help you gather information about the interests of potential program participants and provide information that can help with collection development. You may also use this type of voting-based program to help you identify possible types of books or authors for larger events, such as author visit programs.

NOTES

1. University of Illinois Extension Agency, "Get Up and Move! Intercultural Games," Family Activity Sheet, https://my.extension.illinois.edu/documents/8092503090309/S202family.pdf.

2. The Canadian Association for Health, Physical Education, Recreation, and Dance, "Multi-Cultural Games," *The Clipboard* 4, no. 1, www.phecanada.ca/sites/default/files/multicultural_games_clipboard.pdf.

3. Intersecting Ojibwe Art Curriculum, "Birchbark Wiigwaas Triangle and Ball Game," http://intersectingart.umn.edu/?lesson/65.

4. Wendy Devlin, "History of the *Piñata*," Mexconnect, www.mexconnect.com/articles/459-history-of-the-pi%C3%B1ata.

5. "8 Really Fun Paper and Pencil Math Games," *Wild About Math!* (blog), http://wildaboutmath.com/2008/01/14/8-really-fun-paper-and-pencil-math-games/.

6. Tangram Channel, "History of the Tangram Puzzle," www.tangram-channel.com/history-of-the-tangram/.

7. Tangle Creations, www.tanglecreations.com/.

8. PCGamesN, "The Best Sandbox Games on PC," www.pcgamesn.com/15-best-sandbox-games-pc.

9. Legend Diaries, "Definition of Open World, Free Roaming and Sandbox," March 19, 2016, www.legenddiaries.com/special-features/difference-between-sanbox-and-open-world-games/.

10. Rube Goldberg Machines, "Rube Tube," https://www.rubegoldberg.com/rube-tube/.

11. Dr. Jean Feldman, "Hello and Good Bye Lyrics," http://drjean.org/html/lyrics/lyricsHelloGoodBye.pdf.

12. Rebecca Baker, "Herman the Worm," https://www.youtube.com/watch?v=gmBJ7pS2yYw.

Handouts and Resources

Handouts from this appendix are available at **alaeditions.org/webextras.**

Program Scheduling Survey

(Public Library Name)

(Logo)

Child's name _____

Age and grade _____

E-mail address _____

Parent/guardian name _____

Thank you for sharing your program interests with the library! Please take a moment to let us know about your child's availability for programs as well as what topics your child would like to see covered in a program during fall break this year.

1. Please check all times and days of the week listed below that your child would be available to attend a program at the library during fall break.

   ☐ Mondays at 10:00 a.m.   ☐ Mondays at 2:00 p.m.

   ☐ Tuesdays at 10:00 a.m.   ☐ Tuesdays at 2:00 p.m.

   ☐ Wednesdays at 10:00 a.m.   ☐ Wednesdays at 2:00 p.m.

   ☐ Thursdays at 10:00 a.m.   ☐ Thursdays at 2:00 p.m.

   ☐ Fridays at 10:00 a.m.   ☐ Fridays at 2:00 p.m.

2. Please share topics of interest that your child would like to see as a library program during one of the program times chosen above. The youth services staff will look at the suggestions from this survey and do our best to align programs with the interests of participants.

_____

_____

_____

_____

_____

_____

_____

Program Interest Survey

1. What grade are you (or your child) in?

☐ Kindergarten   ☐ Third, fourth, or fifth grade

☐ First or second grade   Please list your age_____

2. Please rate your level of interest for each of the following programs:

Clubs (crafts or interest groups)

Not interested ☐   ☐   ☐   ☐   ☐   ☐   ☐ Very interested

If you are interested in clubs, please list the type(s) of club(s) you are interested in attending at the library.

_____

_____

Discussion Groups (book discussion, conversation, etc.)

Not interested ☐   ☐   ☐   ☐   ☐   ☐   ☐ Very interested

Gaming or Technology

Not interested ☐   ☐   ☐   ☐   ☐   ☐   ☐ Very interested

Story-Based Program

Not interested ☐   ☐   ☐   ☐   ☐   ☐   ☐ Very interested

Author or Guest Visit

Not interested ☐   ☐   ☐   ☐   ☐   ☐   ☐ Very interested

STEAM (Science, Technology, Engineering, Art, Math)

Not interested ☐   ☐   ☐   ☐   ☐   ☐   ☐ Very interested

(Continued on reverse)

Readers' Theater

Not interested ☐   ☐   ☐   ☐   ☐   ☐   ☐ Very interested

Play-Based Program (dramatic play, play groups, etc.)

Not interested ☐   ☐   ☐   ☐   ☐   ☐   ☐ Very interested

3. Please list any other type of program that you are interested in attending at the library.

_____

_____

4. Please list days and times that you would like to see programs for your age or grade level.

_____

_____

5. Please mark any of the following types of programs that you or your child attends anywhere else in the community. For those marked, please list the specific program and location.

Clubs _____

Discussion Groups _____

Gaming or Technology _____

Story-Based Program _____

Author or Guest Visit _____

STEAM _____

Readers' Theater _____

Play-Based Program _____

6. Please share anything else you would like to tell us about programs at the library.

_____

_____

_____

Patron Large Event Interest Survey

Please mark any subject areas that your family might like to see at a large event sponsored by the library. If you do not see an event on the list, please mark "other" and write in the type of program you would like to suggest.

- ☐ Local Artists
- ☐ Local History and Culture
- ☐ Puppet Performers
- ☐ Musician Performance
- ☐ Magician Performance
- ☐ Martial Arts
- ☐ Theater Performers
- ☐ Dance Performance
- ☐ Video Gaming
- ☐ Health and Fitness

- ☐ Sports Teams
- ☐ Storytellers
- ☐ Outdoor Sports
- ☐ Animals
- ☐ Cooking/Food
- ☐ Science
- ☐ Author Visit
- ☐ Comedy Performance
- ☐ Other: _____

_____

Please mark the days and times that would work best for your family to attend a large event sponsored by the library.

- ☐ Mornings
- ☐ Afternoons
- ☐ Evenings

- ☐ Mondays
- ☐ Tuesdays
- ☐ Wednesdays
- ☐ Thursdays
- ☐ Fridays
- ☐ Saturdays
- ☐ Sundays

Please include any information you would like to provide regarding times and dates of school-sponsored sporting events, extracurricular activities, or school vacation periods when your family would not be available to attend a large event sponsored by the library.

_____

_____

_____

Thank you for taking the time to complete this brief survey. We appreciate your helping the library plan future large events that will best meet the needs and interests of families and children in our community.

Staff Program Planning Process Survey

Please score each area on a scale from 1 to 10 (10 being the best) regarding how you feel the staff worked as a team on the large event planning process.

	Working to meet the interests of our community
	Collaborating with community partners
	Appropriate choice of venue for the type of event
	Clear and realistic deadlines for staff
	Clear and realistic assignments for staff
	Communication of goals, adjustments, and plans
	Preparing materials
	Promoting event to the public
	Helping other staff members as needed
	Meeting the needs of the presenter(s)
	Meeting the needs of the public
	Remaining flexible to meet challenges

Please list the detail(s) that worked best for the staff members on the team.

_____

_____

Please list any areas of concern or areas that need to be improved prior to our next large event.

_____

_____

On a scale of 1 to 10 (10 being the best), what score would you give our team in successfully working together to make this program the best possible for our patrons? _____

Please share any additional comments you have regarding the large event planning process.

_____

_____

_____

Large Event Presentation Agreement

This presentation agreement is entered into between the _____

Public Library and Presenter(s) _____

_____

on (date)_____.

The date and time of the presentation: _____

Presenter(s): _____

_____

Location/Venue: _____

Title of Program: _____

Length of Program: _____ Target Audience Age: _____

Please list any specific needs for the presentation (include technology needs,

personal needs, equipment needs). _____

_____

_____

Presentation Fees and Travel Expenses: _____

Cancellation Agreement: In the event of cancellation due to unforeseen circumstances, such as weather, the event will/will not be rescheduled. Prior cancella-
tions for other reasons made by the library or presenter will be made _____
days in advance. Any fees paid to the presenter will be refunded to the library by
_____ days after cancellation.

Signatures and Contact Information

Presenter: _____ Library Rep. _____

Date _____ Date_____

Phone _____ Phone _____

E-mail _____ E-mail _____

Return Form to: _____ by _____

Large Event Program Planning Checklist

BEFORE THE PROGRAM

☐ Develop budget

☐ Research possible presenters

☐ Contact performers for fee estimate

☐ Obtain guest presenter fee approval from director or board

☐ Reserve venue needed for program (with ample parking and seating)

☐ Make any travel, lodging, or dining reservations needed by the presenter

☐ Send presentation agreement to performer with deadline and method of returning form

☐ Plan promotional materials (print, media, social media, billboards, outreach)

☐ Update presenter on registration numbers, any changes in venue or agreement

☐ Send out reminders to venue, community, and presenter as the event date approaches

☐ Send out press release to local media (television news, radio, newspaper, etc.)

DAY OF THE PROGRAM

☐ Update staff involved in the program about specific assignments during the program

☐ Do final check-in with venue and performer about any new needs or changes

☐ Post any signs or posters around community with directions to the venue if necessary

☐ Send a reminder invitation to media and community through social media

☐ Secure any areas of special parking needed during the event

☐ Contact presenter with information about time and place to meet before the program

☐ Pull together materials that may be needed during the program

☐ Print out registration sheet if registration is required for attendance

☐ Assign staff to keep track of the number of participants (paper or hand clicker)

☐ Assign staff to greet participants and give directions at the door of the venue

- [ ] Greet presenter; assign staff to make sure the presenter has everything needed for the performance during the program

- [ ] Greet program participants at the door (reference registration list if required)

- [ ] Seat program participants in the best seating pattern for easy flow and best arrangement for easy viewing

- [ ] Make announcements at the start of the event (information about the presenters, the building exits, where restrooms are located, and what will happen at the close of the performance)

- [ ] Observe the audience for any needs that might arise during the performance

- [ ] Take pictures of the audience and presenter during the show (be sure to obtain photo permission)

- [ ] Make any adjustments needed during the program wrap-up

- [ ] At the close of the program, thank the presenter and announce information about the presenter's future projects and appearances

- [ ] Manage the flow of participants exiting the venue

- [ ] Manage the flow of parking traffic around the venue

- [ ] Clean the venue area

- [ ] Check for straggling program attendees in restrooms and other areas before closing venue

- [ ] Offer the presenter help with loading any materials into a vehicle or transport

DEBRIEFING

- [ ] Schedule staff meeting with all staff who assisted with the large event (within the week after the event)

- [ ] During the meeting, discuss the details that ran smoothly and the details that need to be reviewed and adjusted before the library's next large event

- [ ] Ask staff to complete an evaluation of the event planning process, the quality of the presentation, and how successfully the staff worked together on the program as a project

- [ ] Document the number of attendees and any comments you received from those in attendance

- [ ] Document the amount of money spent on the program (including presenter fees, materials costs, and any other program costs)

- [ ] Present information about the success of the program to the library director and board

Special Needs Program Survey

Does your child have any specific sensory needs that are impacted by lighting? If yes, please explain.

_____

_____

_____

_____

Does your child have any specific needs that are impacted by noises or the volume of sounds? If yes, please explain.

_____

_____

_____

_____

Does your child have any special physical needs that impact sitting or moving? If yes, please explain.

_____

_____

_____

_____

Are there any other special considerations that would help your child or family attend a program at the library? Please explain.

_____

_____

_____

_____

_____

Press Release Template

FOR IMMEDIATE RELEASE

Title of Program or Event and Name of Library

Date of Press Release

City, STATE—[Insert four to six paragraphs about the program. Include a brief summary of the program specifying date, time, and location. Include information about the number of sessions if the program has more than one. Include quotes from library board members, community members, or previous program participants that help promote the program to potentially interested members of the community.]

   For more information, call the library at [phone number] or visit the library's website at [web address].

Contact Person's Name
Library Address
Phone Number
E-mail Address

Index

CPSIA information can be obtained
at www.ICGtesting.com
Printed in the USA
BVHW011151010222
627768BV00010B/173